... love from

Brian & Marianne

THE GOD WHO ANSWERS PRAYER

by Brian Spicer

Revised Edition November 2024

One generation will commend your works to another;
they will tell of your mighty deeds.
(Psalm 145:4)

Introduction

This is not an autobiography, but a simple recounting of some of the remarkable ways in which God has so lovingly led us and provided for us for more than half a century. Great is his faithfulness!

It consists of messages given on eight successive Sundays during the summer of 2023, plus two brief appendices I wrote earlier.

I would like to dedicate these pages to my beloved wife, Marianne, my dear children, Kathryn, Stephanie, Amy, Timothy & Emily, and my precious grandchildren, Naomi, Joseph & Fiona. I owe you so much and love you so dearly.

Cincinnati, November 2024

Many thanks to Tom Hohenstatt, who helped me in so many ways.

THE GOD WHO ANSWERS PRAYER

Chapter One

July 30, 2023

Throughout the years, as I've shared various examples of God's leading and provision, different ones have urged me to write them down, especially my son, Tim, who keeps checking up on me to see whether I'm working on it or not.

It all takes time, and I wondered whether I could use the time I normally spend on preparing the weekly sermons to write down these remarkable answers to prayer, and share them with you week by week.

A number of you have heard some of these accounts before. I hope you will bear with me.

All the glory belongs to God. I can hardly believe that the God who created and sustains the universe would take me, a very insecure young man, living in a rather poor neighborhood, and lead me and provide for me the way he has.

Rosalind Goforth (1864-1942) saw many answers to prayer when she and her husband were missionaries in China, but she said, "This doesn't mean that we haven't failed in many ways, because we have." I want to echo that. The Lord has been very gracious to me, answering so many prayers in such remarkable ways, but that doesn't mean I haven't failed in many ways, because, sad to say, I have.

This testimony really begins in the summer of 1969. I had just turned 23 (I was born on June 4, 1946) and had just returned to my childhood home in Huyton (pronounced *Highton*), Liverpool, England after completing my college education in Stafford. I was very happy to be home again with my widowed mother, Dorothy May Spicer, my younger brother, Douglas, and my older sister, Audrey, who worked in Norway during the summer months and in Liverpool during the rest of the year. Our sister, June Vernon, and her family lived just around the corner.

I was also very happy to be a part of Page Moss Lane Baptist Church again. I had attended its afternoon Sunday School since my early childhood, and it was there that I first heard the gospel.

When I was about 14 I knelt by my bed and asked Jesus Christ to be my Savior. A year or so later I was baptized in the presence of my family and school friends, whom I had invited. I was so grateful I could testify to those who knew me best that I was now a follower of the Lord Jesus Christ.

Going back to the summer of 1969, one of my good friends at the church, Joan Howson, now Joan Smith, spent a couple of weeks on an outreach in the south of England run by a group called Project Evangelism. When she came back, I could see a big change in her. She was no longer shy, but an outgoing witness for the Lord. She told me they had gone door to door, and even into pubs, inviting people to the nightly evangelistic meetings, and that many had attended and quite a few had received the Lord as their Savior. She said to me, "Brian, you *have* to go next year!"

I felt I could never do what she had done, and simply dismissed the idea. Some months later she said, "Brian, I'm still praying you'll go on that outreach in the summer." I thought, "Well, if she's praying about it, then the least I should do is pray about it too." As I prayed, I felt I should go. I applied to Project Evangelism and was accepted.

I counted the number of days till the beginning of the outreach and found it was exactly 100. I thought that if I would get up an hour earlier each day and pray about the outreach, I would have 100 hours of prayer behind me before setting off. It was during those times of prayer that the Lord began preparing me for all that lay ahead.

During that time, a lady in our neighborhood asked my mother if she would go on vacation with her to Spain. My mother answered, "Only if Brian goes with us." However, I was already fully committed to going on the outreach, and said to my poor mother, "If I would go to another country, I would never go to a hot country like Spain." (Little did I know that within a few months I would be living in Spain – and that it would be one of the greatest experiences of my life – or that I would spend almost all of the rest of my life living in countries much hotter than England.) Audrey invited her to Norway. It was our mother's only trip abroad, and she thoroughly enjoyed it.

Finally, the time came for me to join the outreach in Dewsbury, Yorkshire, 65 miles east of Liverpool. It was the last week of July and the first week of August 1970.

In the mornings we went door to door inviting people to the evangelistic meetings, which were held each evening at the Town Hall. In the afternoons the leaders gave *us* challenging messages. Each evening some of the team members conducted the evangelistic meeting, while the rest of us went to the basement and prayed earnestly that many would respond to the Lord. Then we would be called up to pray with those who had gone forward.

One evening I was asked to pray with a 12-year-old boy called Andrew. He told me he only had sixpence on him, and if he caught the next bus, it would take him directly to his village for sixpence, but if he caught the bus after that, it would take him on a round-about route and would cost him ninepence. I didn't realize what he was trying to say, otherwise I would've gladly given him the threepence he needed. He stayed and prayed to receive the Lord as his Savior. As we came out of the room, there on the floor was a threepenny bit, a coin worth three old pence. He excitedly picked it up and "went on his way rejoicing." (This was six months before the old currency, which had 240 old pennies to the pound, was replaced by the new currency, which has 100 new pence to the pound.)

This was the first time I saw the Lord's miraculous provision of the exact amount needed. It impressed me very much and I have never forgotten it.

One of the leaders of the outreach in Dewsbury was an older man, Alf Ridpath, who spoke to us about the spiritual needs of countries like India and Turkey. I was shocked to hear that there were only about 50 born-again Christians in Turkey, which had a population of 35 million at the time.

During one session, we were challenged to "go into all the world and preach the gospel." As I was listening, I experienced something for the first time, which I have since experienced on a number of other occasions. I felt that the Lord was speaking directly to me, not through what the speaker was saying, and not audibly, but inwardly. I felt he was saying to *me*, and *only* to me, "When the appeal is made, I don't want you to go forward. I have other plans for you. I will lead you as I led Abraham, who went out not knowing where he was going." 19 people went forward. Then the leaders told us that they had prayed, "Lord, if you want us to form a missionary society, let exactly 19 people go forward, not more, not less." I don't know why they chose the number 19.

I arrived back home on Saturday, August 8. The following day I told my mother, who was not yet saved, that I was planning to give in my notice the next day. She was worried because I was going to give up my well-paid job as a design engineer without knowing what lay ahead.

As soon as I arrived at work on Monday morning, I asked my boss' secretary if I could speak to him. She told me he wouldn't be in till Wednesday.

Meanwhile, the next day, Tuesday, August 11, Joan asked me if I would like to go with her to a meeting that evening in Netherley, a part of Liverpool I had never been to before. Much to my surprise, Alf Ridpath was there. After the meeting he said to me, "Well, Brian, what's the Lord doing in *your* life?"

I told him I was going to give in my notice the next morning, but didn't know anything beyond that. He asked me when my notice would be up. I answered, "I guess on September 11." He immediately told me, "On September 14 an Operation Mobilization conference begins in St. Mary Cray, and I think you should go to it." I had never heard of Operation Mobilization (usually known by its initials O. M., generally just written OM) or St. Mary Cray.

The following morning I gave in my notice. Alf had told me to call Derek Virgin (a former professional soccer player) to ask him if I could attend the conference. Derek told me I could, but I wouldn't be able to join one of the year teams, because I hadn't been on an OM summer team. He sent me a package of books, which I had to read before attending the conference.

One of them was *True Discipleship* by William MacDonald. In it he quoted the words of Jesus, "Anyone who loves his father or mother more than me is not worthy of me" (Matthew 10:37). My dear father, Albert Spicer, had died 13 years earlier when I was 11 years old. I loved my mother, and was very happy to be living with her and my siblings again. I had a great struggle in my soul, and even cried, as I realized the Lord was calling me to leave my home and family, and yet I knew I had to put him before them. Jesus promised, "No one who has left home or brothers or sisters or mother or father or children or fields for me and the gospel will fail to receive a hundred times as much in this present age (homes, brothers, sisters, mothers, children and fields – and with them, persecutions) and in the age to come, eternal life" (Mark 10:29-30).

On Sunday, September 13, 1970 my family accompanied me downtown as I set off by train, first to London and then on to St. Mary Cray, just a few miles south-east of central London. The conference was five weeks long. Everyone else had been on an OM summer team and knew other people, but I didn't know anyone. The messages were very challenging, calling us to yield every part of our lives to the Lordship of Christ. I felt very insecure and out of my depth, but the Lord was using these messages to prepare me to serve him.

My sister, Audrey, came to visit me. I think she wanted to make sure I wasn't involved in a cult. Usually the meetings were very serious, but that evening (and I think *only* that evening) George Verwer, the founder of Operation Mobilization, had us laughing a lot, which did us all the world of good. Audrey enjoyed it and went home to reassure everyone.

At that time OM had the policy of not making any needs known to anyone – except to God. For a number of years they had been praying that God would provide a ship for them to go port to port with the gospel, and during the conference one had become available for £70,000.

The main meetings were over at nine o'clock in the evening, but then the prayer meetings began, often going into the early hours of the morning, even though we all had to be up again at 6:30. Each day we were told how much money was now available towards the purchase of the ship, and how much was still needed. It was exciting to see God answering prayer, and on the day the payment had to be made, the final amount needed was received. From this I learned that we don't have to tell others our needs. We just need to tell God.

It was the last week of the conference and I didn't know what would come next. Then I received a note from Jonathan McRostie, one of the leaders of OM, saying he wanted to see me. I felt very apprehensive as I went to see him, but, much to my surprise, he told me that he had spoken to my small group leader at the conference and to my pastor in Liverpool and that he wanted to offer me a place on one of the teams that year.

He asked me which country I would like to go to. I immediately said, "Turkey," but he said, "No, go to one of the countries in Europe." At that time OM Europe had teams in Austria, Belgium, France, Italy and Spain.

After the meetings were over that evening, I got alone and asked God to guide me. It got really late and I was very tired when I came across David's words, "Let the morning bring me word of your unfailing love, for I have put my trust in you. Show me the way I should go, for to you I lift up my soul" (Psalm 143:8). I felt I should go to bed and that God would show me in the morning. When I got up, without even realizing that Spain was mentioned in the Bible, and only in one passage at that, I turned to Romans 15, where Paul speaks of his desire to visit Spain, and I knew that God had shown me where I should go. The OM Spain team leader kindly accepted me on to his team.

After the conference, those living in Britain and Europe could go home for a week. Then the teams set off from Zaventem, close to Brussels, Belgium. I hadn't met any of the other team members, but they all knew each other to some extent, because they had all attended the daily meetings for those going to Spain. As we traveled through France, a Mexican young man, Willy Peña, noticed my quietness and asked me why I had joined the team. As I shared how the Lord had led me, he said, "Yes, you definitely belong on this team."

I had only been in Spain for three weeks when I received a telegram from Audrey saying that our mother was dying and that I should come home. I immediately flew from Madrid to London (my first-ever flight), then took a train from London to Liverpool and finally a bus to Whiston Hospital, where I had been born All the way I was quietly praying that I would have one more opportunity to share the gospel with my mother. I had prayed for her for ten years, ever since I had come to know the Lord myself. During the previous months the two of us had had a number of conversations about the Lord, and she had begun attending church with me. When I arrived at the hospital she woke up and we spent about an hour together. I asked her if she wanted to receive the Lord as her Savior and she said, "Yes." After we prayed she slipped into a four-day-long coma before dying. During that time my sister, June, said that she also wanted to ask the Lord to save her. June remained faithful to the Lord for the remaining twenty-two years of her life.

On the day of my mother's funeral the electricity workers went on strike. It was cold and dark in the house, so I went to bed early.

As I sat in bed, with my Bible in one hand and a candle in the other, I asked the Lord to show me whether my mother was truly saved or not. I felt that the Lord was urging me to read Isaiah 66, a chapter I wasn't familiar with.

There I read, "Rejoice with [her], and be glad with her, all you who love her. Rejoice for joy with her, all you who mourn for her. ... For thus says the Lord, Behold, I will extend peace to her like a river, and ... glory ... like a flowing stream. ... As one whom his mother comforts, so I will comfort you, and you shall be comforted. ... When you see this, your heart shall rejoice."

The passage is actually speaking about the city of Jerusalem, but I felt that the Lord was reassuring me that my mother was safe with him in heaven.

It was the end of November, and Audrey asked me not to go back to Spain until the Christmas and New Year holidays were over. In early January 1971 I returned to Madrid. It was the coldest winter in a hundred years, and there was almost no heating in the house, but the Lord helped us all to have a good attitude. (One thing that was emphasized in the OM conferences was not to complain.)

During my time in Spain, one answer to prayer stands out above all the rest:

Most days the team went door to door in Madrid (and occasionally in the surrounding villages) selling Christian books and Bibles. An English fellow, Geoff Bone, visited our team for a short while. One mealtime he said, "If anyone would like to sell more books, join me in the living room after the meal."

An English girl, Judith Meldrum (who was fluent in Spanish), and I (only a beginner) were the only two who stayed to meet with him. Geoff asked us how much money we usually sold for, and we told him it was around 65 pesetas. He encouraged us to pray that we would sell 100 pesetas' worth of books. Once that had happened, he suggested we should pray for 150 pesetas' worth, and so on in increments of 50 pesetas.

At some point Geoff returned to England, but I kept praying I could sell more books (so that more people could hear the message of salvation), and God kept answering. No one else knew anything about this.

One day a group of us went to a village outside Madrid, and by that time I was praying I would sell 700 pesetas' worth of books.

After a few hours I had sold for more than 500 pesetas, and there was only one more door I could knock on. I stopped and prayed. A young man came to the door and I showed him my books. He said, "I'll take one of each," which was the only time that ever happened to me. So God answered my prayer.

On the return journey, one of the team members began asking each of us how much we had sold for. I was hoping he wouldn't ask me, but he did. When I told him, he was stunned. He had a degree in Spanish from a prestigious university, and a few months earlier I hadn't known a word of Spanish.

One of our team leaders, Filip from Sweden, asked me to give a summary of the book of Deuteronomy the following week. I read it through once to re-familiarize myself with it, and then a second time taking notes. It was the first Bible Study I ever led.

A wonderful summer of outreach was spent in the province of Granada in the south of Spain. Jack Rendel, the team leader there, invited me to join his team after the OM conference in London, and I was very open to doing this. However, during a brief visit home just before the conference, my pastor asked me to consider staying in Liverpool to go door to door in the area around our church.

So I began to pray, "Lord, is it Granada or is it Liverpool?"

On the first day of my second conference, in September 1971, the speaker for the first session wasn't able to be there. So someone asked if one of the team leaders would come forward and present the country he was working in. Virgil Amos, an outgoing African American from California, spoke about Iran. My heart was stirred and I began to pray, "Lord, is it Iran rather than Spain or England?" After a while I realized I was no longer praying about England. One day I bumped into Jack and said, "I'm not sure whether I should go to Granada or to Iran." He said, "Go to Iran." He then told me that he had once been on an OM Iran team and was praying that God would raise up workers to go there. I looked on a world map to see where Iran was. I was amazed to see it was as far from England as New York was. To me, at that time, New York seemed to be at the ends of the earth.

The overland journey to Iran took a week, driving slowly in a convoy day and night. We traveled through Belgium, Germany, Austria, what was then Yugoslavia (now Slovenia, Croatia and Serbia), and then Bulgaria, Turkey and into Iran. It was an amazing experience.

My first year in Iran was very difficult and I began to shake. (I had first noticed this weakness when I was a young teenager, and then again during my third year of college, when I realized that I didn't want to be an engineer. Back then I could hardly lift up a cup of tea to my lips or put a forkful of food into my mouth.)

Virgil started public speaking classes. Each person on the "boys' team" had to prepare and deliver a short sermon. I said to Virgil, "I know I will never speak in public," and asked to be excused. Eleven years later he told me, "You were the only one I ever excused, and you were the only one who became a pastor."

Various members of the team were sent to different parts of the country to live and work with Iranian pastors or foreign missionaries. I was sent to an elderly Iranian pastor and his wife in the city of Ahvaz, about 500 miles south-west of our team house in Tehran. It was extremely hot, and they barely gave me anything to eat. During the time I was with them I lost a lot of weight. I can only presume they were destitute of funds.

When I returned to England I only weighed 8 stone (112 pounds) and I was still struggling with shaking.

I felt there was no way I could return to Iran, so I didn't go to the conference, which was in Birmingham, not London, that year.

Virgil called me and asked me to come for the last couple of days of the conference.

He said I would be able to see everyone before they returned to Iran. I felt I could do that.

When I arrived, Virgil told me he had arranged for George Verwer to speak with me. George and I spoke for quite a long time, which was very good of him seeing he had so many responsibilities at the conference. He told me Virgil really wanted me to go back to Iran, and that he himself had no objection to my going back. I was amazed. No other mission leader would have said that.

One of the team members, Chris Pyle, invited me to join him for the weekend at his parents' home in Teignmouth, Devon. Chris' pastor, William Coffin, had been the pastor of my church in Liverpool when I was a young teenager, and I thought it would be nice to see him and his wife again.

A young man called Bob, who was on the OM France team, invited Chris and me to spend the night at his home on our way down to Devon. I think it was somewhere in rural Gloucestershire.

It was an impressive 17th century house, set on 500 acres of farmland, with peacocks on the lawn. Bob's parents welcomed us and showed us the bed where John Wesley used to sleep whenever he was in the area. Everyone was very kind to me.

I asked Chris not to tell the Coffins I would be at the church the next day. I wanted to surprise them. Mr. Coffin spoke on 1 Corinthians 1:27-29 – "God chose the foolish things of the world to shame the wise; God chose the weak things of the world to shame the strong. He chose the lowly things of this world and the despised things – and the things that are not – to nullify the things that are, so that no one may boast before him."

During the sermon he mentioned that he had prepared the message on Tuesday, which was before Virgil had called me. Mr. Coffin didn't know I would be there, yet every word was just for me. Due to my shaking, I had been feeling very foolish, weak, lowly and despised for quite some time, but I now felt that God was showing me to go back to Iran.

On the return journey to Iran I began to feel stronger and healthier, and the shaking stopped. We went straight down to the Persian Gulf, where OM's ship, the *Logos*, was visiting. It was a joy to help out there.

Most of that year, like the previous one, was spent going door to door selling Christian books and scriptures in Tehran. At that time there was religious freedom under the Shah (the king of Iran), and what we were doing was legal.

However, many ardent Moslems felt that it had to be, or ought to be, illegal, and so they would call the police.

One day I was arrested and told I was going to be deported immediately. I asked if I could make a phone call. Virgil (who liked to drive fast) told me that he would meet the train in Tabriz (about 400 miles away) and give me enough money to get back to England, which he did.

Two armed guards sat with me until we reached the Turkish border, where they turned me over to an Iranian official, who wrote in Persian (which uses Arabic script) in red ink on the photo in my passport that I would never be allowed back into Iran.

When I arrived home I shared with my friends at the church what had happened, and asked them to pray whether I should try to go back to Iran or not. Understandably, they were not too sure what to say or do.

The OM conference was approaching, and I felt sure the Lord would show me what to do while I was there.

The new team leader felt that the decision was between the Lord and me. When I went to the passport office, the official just laughed at the red "scribble" on my photo, and before long I had a new passport.

On the last day of the conference George Verwer addressed all who were still unsure whether to go out with a team that year. He suggested asking the Lord to provide a certain amount of money if he wanted us to go. He mentioned different amounts for different countries. For Iran he suggested £90.

On the bus back to Liverpool I quietly prayed, "Lord, if you want me to go back to Iran, please provide £90. I won't express any doubt about my going back, and I won't let anyone know I need a penny. It's just between you and me."

The next day at church, as people shook hands with me they slipped a £1 note or a £5 note into my hand without saying a word. This was remarkable, because for the 7 years I was with OM, although the church sent £180 a year for my support, for which I was very grateful, this was the only time I received any personal gifts like this.

A few days later I bumped into a dear friend, Lionel Watkins, who belonged to another church. Suddenly he said, "I feel the Lord wants me to give you this £5 note."

On my last evening I counted up all I had, and it came to £85 and a few coins. I packed my suitcase, and the following morning said goodbye to Audrey and Doug as they left for work.

There were still a couple of hours before I had to leave. I prayed, "Lord, probably nobody knows I'm still here, and nobody knows I'm lacking £5, but you know everything. I'm totally willing to go back to Iran if that's your will, and I am totally willing to stay here if that's your will, but I won't go back to Iran unless you provide the last £5."

A few minutes before I had to leave, the telephone rang. It was Audrey. She said, "I've been thinking. Maybe you need some socks or underwear. There's a £5 note in my drawer. Just take it." I thanked her, and grabbed my suitcase. I ran to the bus stop and just caught the bus downtown. Then I ran into the station, bought my ticket and jumped on the train to London just before it left. The Lord had showed me I should return to Iran.

Six years later, Audrey came to visit us. When I told her that God had answered my prayer through her, tears came to her eyes.

All praise to the living God, who leads his people and provides for them.

Amen.

THE GOD WHO ANSWERS PRAYER

Chapter Two

August 6, 2023

Marianne (pronounced *Marianna*) from Germany, who was to become the love of my life, had just joined the team. On the journey to Iran, we all spent the night at the lovely home of her parents, Gustav & Betty Rink, in the Black Forest. They had been missionaries in China and knew English well. This was my first meeting with my future parents-in-law, who would so lovingly take the place of my deceased parents.

When we reached the Iranian border, the official looked at my passport and said, "Come on in, the British are our friends!" Unknown to me, Britain and Iran had just signed a treaty of friendship!

In January 1974, our new team leader, Ron George, sent me to represent OM Iran at an OM Middle East conference in Beirut, Lebanon. The OM Lebanon team leader, John Ferwerda, gave a six-hour-long testimony of God's faithfulness to him, three hours the first evening, and three the next.

It was so thrilling, and, to some extent, an inspiration for the testimony I am now sharing with you.

Then Ron sent me to India for three months (April-June 1974), where I traveled extensively. About half of my time in India was spent at the headquarters of Brother Bakht Singh in Hyderabad, Andhra Pradesh. Brother Bakht Singh (1903-2000) "was India's foremost evangelist, preacher and indigenous church planter." He was very kind to me.

All the travel was overland in those days, and I felt very privileged to see such wonderful places.

During the summer of 1974, I was supposed to spend one night at Marianne's parents' home. A team was supposed to arrive the next day to drop off Marianne and pick me up to go on to Sweden, where we would spend ten days sharing about OM with the churches there. However, the team's van had broken down in a remote part of Turkey and it took a week for the garage to get the part and fix it. So I spent eight days with Marianne's parents and two sisters, Ilse and Christa, who also knew English well. It was all part of God's plan for my future in-laws and me to get to know one another.

My final three years with OM (1974-77) were spent in Tabriz, the capital of the province of Azerbaijan in northwest Iran. (This is different from, and south of, the present-day country of Azerbaijan, which was then a part of the USSR.) The people were Turkish Iranians and the local language was Turkish. However, almost all of the people knew Persian well, because all education and media had to be in the national language.

The Presbyterian Church of Tabriz, founded by American missionaries in the early 19th century, had asked OM to send them a team to help with the children and youth. The church was made up mainly of families from the Assyrian and Armenian Christian minority groups, with just a few individuals from the Turkish majority. Malcolm Steer led the team. His Persian was very good. He and his wife, Ann, both from a Plymouth Brethren background, were from Bristol, England.

I had only been in Tabriz for a few months when I was asked to accompany a group of new OMers to Kuwait to renew their visas. The night before I set off to join them in Tehran, I was struck by these words from Psalm 118:17-18 "I will not die but live, and will proclaim what the Lord has done. The Lord has ... not given me over to death."

We had to drive the almost 600 miles from Tehran to Abadan on Ashura, the most fanatical day of mourning in the Islamic year. Normally foreigners didn't venture out of their homes on this day, but we kept driving through towns and villages where there were processions of men flogging themselves with heavy chains.

In Abadan we paid to have a wooden boat take the 13 of us (including a baby) and our two vans across the Persian Gulf to Kuwait. We were told to be at the dock early the next morning, which we were. We traveled a few miles down the Shatt al-Arab river, which separates Iran and Iraq. Then the anchor was put down and the captain went ashore in a longboat. We were stranded in the middle of the wide river for several days. The sailors kept assuring us, "The captain will come soon."

Finally, he came just as darkness was falling and told us we would set off. The boat had only one oil lamp, so I said to him, "We've waited all this time. Why not wait till morning? We wouldn't want to be struck by another boat." But he just laughed it off.

Where the river turns into the Gulf there was a customs ship, where we had to show our passports.

Then Glen Garner, from Oregon, told me, "This morning I felt the Lord was telling me I would pray for someone today and the person would be healed, but no one has mentioned any health problems." I told him that the captain had said he had pain in his side. We went to him and asked if he would like us to pray for him. We told him we would pray in the name of Jesus Christ. He agreed. Glen prayed in English and I translated into Persian. Then we lay down to sleep.

Suddenly we were struck by another boat, which didn't stay around to help. There was a big hole below the waterline and water was gushing in. The sailors kept lamenting, "My wife will be a widow and my children will be fatherless," but didn't do anything to help, except for one man who operated the bilge pump. We had to throw the cargo overboard until the hole was above the waterline.

Then the boat returned to the customs ship. The captain shouted to the customs officers, "These men are prophets. They said this would happen. And they prayed for me and I was healed." Then, one by one, the customs officers asked for prayer, some for healing and some for other things.

The Lord had not given us over to death! Praise his name!

The three years I spent in Tabriz were very happy ones, teaching the children and youth, conducting home Bible Studies and doing some bookselling in the city and surrounding areas. I'm sure the Lord must have answered many other prayers while I was in Tabriz, but I would just like to share the following:

On one occasion some OMers passed through Tabriz on their way home for the annual OM conference. I was supposed to join them, but was too ill to go along.

I had heard that the train from Istanbul to Paris, the famed Orient Express, only left once a week, but I had no idea when. I prayed that the Lord would heal me and show me when to begin my journey. One morning I felt that the Lord was prompting me to leave right then. I caught a bus to the Turkish border. Someone there asked me if I wanted to go Erzurum, the first major city in eastern Turkey. He had one place left in his minivan. From Erzurum I caught a bus to Istanbul, a journey of more than 750 miles. I arrived just 1½ hours before the train's departure, just enough time to get from the bus station to the train station and buy some food and drink for the journey. What a kind and loving God we have!

In 1975 we had announced an English-language Christmas Eve service for Tabriz's foreign community.

Malcolm was going to preach, but came down with diphtheria a few hours before the meeting. He said to me, "You'll have to preach." I answered, "But I've never preached a sermon in my life," to which he replied, "You have no choice. You're the only one in the city who knows both the Lord and English."

I prayed that the Lord would show me what to speak on and he did. After the service, Dr. Wilson Lazar, the chief elder of the church, said to me, "I didn't know you could preach! From now on, one Sunday Malcolm preaches and you play the organ; the next Sunday you preach and he plays the organ." And so I began preaching, much to my own amazement.

We preached in English and it was translated into Turkish, which we didn't understand. One Sunday the sermon was translated into Persian for the sake of an Iranian visitor who didn't know Turkish. I was speaking on assurance of salvation. The translator obviously didn't agree with what I was saying and kept changing the message.

After the service Malcolm said, "Well, we'll just have to preach in Persian from now on," which we began to do, even though my Persian wasn't as good as Malcolm's.

When I was young, someone I knew had married against her mother's wishes, and it had not gone well for her. Even though I was only a child, I decided that if I ever wanted to get married and *anyone* would be against it, I would not go ahead.

During my teens I dated a little, but when I was 19 I made a promise to the Lord: "I won't date anyone until you show me she's the one you want me to marry." No one influenced me to do this, nor had I ever heard of anyone making such a promise. Little did I realize that I would go through my entire twenties before finding the one I should marry, but I have no regrets. On the contrary, I am very grateful. I wouldn't have had it any other way.

Operation Mobilization had what they called a "social policy." Everyone was encouraged to devote their first two years with OM to serving the Lord, and not to finding a marriage partner. A single fellow and a single girl were not to have private conversations, but everyone could speak to everyone else in group settings.

If a fellow was interested in a particular girl, he was to share this with the team leader. Then the team leader's wife would ask the girl if she felt the same way. If she didn't, that was the end of it. If she did, then it would be announced to the whole team that they had "social permission," an opportunity to get to know one another.

In the spring of 1975 the OM Iran team had a conference just north of Tehran, and I came down from Tabriz to attend it. One day both Marianne and I had to go into the city for different reasons, and an American young man drove us there. We ended up in a terrible traffic jam, and for about an hour Marianne and I had a delightful conversation, mainly about classical music, which we both love. Marianne says she fell in love with me that day and began asking the Lord if I was the one for her. I never suspected anyone would fall in love with me.

Shortly afterwards my sister Audrey came to visit me in Iran. When she returned to England, June asked her, "Are there any nice girls on the team for Brian?"

She replied, "Well, they were all nice, but there was this one German girl – she was the nicest of them all." I knew nothing of all this.

A few months later, some OMers, including Marianne, spent a night at our team house in Tabriz on their way back to Europe. When they left the next morning, I thought, "It's a pity I didn't get to know Marianne," and I began to ask the Lord if she was the one for me. We hardly knew each other. We had only had one conversation. So I asked the Lord for a sign. I began to pray, "Lord, if you want us to marry, cause us to bump into each other somewhere in this big, wide world."

When Marianne returned to Germany, her sisters asked her if there was anyone she was interested in. When she said, "Brian," they encouraged her to write to me, but she felt she shouldn't be the one to initiate anything. She says she felt a holy fear of doing anything outside of God's will.

So Marianne was in Germany praying about me, and I was in Iran praying about her.

One time, as I was praying, I said to the Lord, "If you would want me never to marry and thereby never to have children, I am willing to accept that." Suddenly an immense feeling of peace and joy flooded my soul.

Shortly after that it was my 30th birthday and someone said to me, "You must feel terrible. You're 30 and not married," to which I replied, "No, I'm enjoying my birthday."

Then in September 1976 Marianne came to an OM conference I was attending in Belgium. She arrived one evening, and the next morning I had to leave for England to attend my sister Audrey's wedding, so we hardly saw each other, and that only in a group setting, but God *had* caused us to bump into each other, as I had prayed.

When I got back to Belgium, Marianne had already returned to Germany.

Then my team leader, Ron George, told me that he wanted me to join him in southern California, recruiting young people for OM. It was a great privilege to do that. I enjoyed the natural beauty of California, and the kindness of many people, but felt out of my depth with the culture there. When I left America, I thought it was unlikely that I would ever return.

Meanwhile, Marianne was asked to go back to Iran to work as a nurse in the Christian Hospital in Esfahan, which was run by the Anglican Church Missionary Society. She had studied pediatric nursing in Schwäbisch Hall and had worked as a nurse in different hospitals in Germany. In Esfahan she was put in charge of a men's ward, which was quite a shock to her, but she loved her men and they loved her.

When I finally returned to Iran, I heard that Marianne had also come back. So I wrote to her, asking if we could get to know one other. The evening before my letter arrived, an English girl asked Marianne if there was anyone she liked, and she told her about me. The next day, when that girl went to pick up the mail, there was a letter for Marianne from me! She ran to give it to her.

Marianne replied immediately, but her letter got lost in the mail for five weeks. I concluded she wasn't interested in me, and she couldn't understand why I hadn't replied to her.

Fortunately, Anni Kane, a dear friend of both of us, went to visit Marianne, and Marianne told her what had happened. Anni called me while Marianne was at work, and everything was quickly sorted out. Soon afterwards, in March 1977, we met at the OM conference in Tehran and were granted Social Permission.

I wrote to Marianne's father asking him if I could marry his daughter. Even though I was 30 and Marianne 26, we wouldn't have proceeded against his wishes. Happily, he wrote back giving his fullest blessing.

A few weeks later we got engaged. In Iran engagement is a formal ceremony followed by a reception. We had two engagement celebrations, one in Esfahan, where Marianne worked, and, four days later, another in Tabriz, where I worked. In both places the lilacs were at their very best, and ever since they have been very special to us.

During the four months of our engagement, we hardly saw each other, because we lived a two days' journey apart, and I, as an OMer, had hardly any money.

We wrote letters, but couldn't really telephone each other, because we knew someone always listened in to our team's calls.

A couple of weeks before our wedding we flew to Germany. We hardly knew each other, but we knew that God had brought us together.

Marianne's mother and sisters had made all the arrangements. We just followed their instructions, which we were very happy to do, and it was basically a stress-free experience. One friend offered to be our photographer, and another our organist.

In German villages, once the church bells begin to ring, the bride and groom walk together to the church, preceded by a small wedding party and followed by all the guests.

The six weeks before our wedding it had rained incessantly and the farmers hadn't been able to harvest their crops. Marianne's mother began talking about making other arrangements in case it would rain on our wedding day.

A few days before the wedding, Marianne and I went for a walk in the Black Forest and were caught in a sudden downpour. Marianne said, "We won't make any other arrangements. We'll just trust the Lord to give us good weather."

I could see that she had total faith the Lord would bless us with a beautiful day, and right then and there we prayed together in the pouring rain.

The day before our church wedding, we had our civil wedding, which is required by German law. It sprinkled a little on that day, but we didn't regard the civil wedding as our real wedding.

That evening I said to Marianne's father, "Good night, Mr. Rink," to which he replied, "You may call me Papa now." My father had died twenty years earlier and my mother seven, and Marianne's parents truly became second parents to me. Her mother now became "Mama" to me too. They were so loving, kind and generous.

Our church wedding took place on Saturday, September 10, 1977. The weather couldn't have been more beautiful, and the sunset was magnificent. God was so good to us.

Marianne's godparents, Samuel & Luise Schulz, were visiting from America. They had been fellow missionaries with Marianne's parents in China, where Marianne was born. Pastor Schulz kindly translated the wedding sermon into English for my family and me.

We stayed at the reception until the last guest left at one o'clock in the morning. We had smiled so much that our faces were aching! We were so grateful for the lovely wedding Mama and Papa had given us.

Esfahan is a beautiful city. Iranians say *Esfahan nesf-e Jahan*, implying that if you've been to *Esfahan*, you've seen *half the world*!

At first I taught English. Then the Bishop of Iran, Hassan Dehqani Tafti, asked me to preach every Sunday in a small church in the Armenian sector of the city. They were dear people. This provided me with a work permit.

And then the young man who had been in charge of the Boys' Hostel returned to America because his mother had been diagnosed with cancer,

Marianne and I were asked to take over. The hostel was not for orphans, but for boys whose families couldn't look after them. When we took over, there were only three boys.

During the summer, while there was no school, we enjoyed refurbishing the building to accommodate up to twelve boys.

As the new school year approached, we received a number of applications.

Each time I conducted an interview, I was quietly asking the Lord whether we should accept that particular boy or not. It seemed that the Lord kept saying, "Not this one. Just trust me." So not long before the first day of school, after turning down a number of boys, we still only had the original three.

But then the Lord sent one boy after another, and the hostel was filled before school began. The youngest was eight and the oldest sixteen. The Lord brought together just the right group of boys. During the first few weeks they tested us, as was only to be expected, but then everything settled down, and there was a happy and peaceful atmosphere in the hostel.

Earlier that summer we had flown to Germany for the wedding of Marianne's sister Ilse to Siegfried Kübler, a young man from the same village.

When we returned to Esfahan, before we deplaned, we said to each other, "This is where we'll spend the rest of our lives, and this is where we'll be buried." We meant it with all our hearts, but it was not meant to be.

An Iranian young man we knew told me, "We have a *qahraman*, that is, a hero, a champion." I asked, "What's his name?" "Khomeini," he said, to which I replied, "I've never heard of him."

But soon we heard all about him, and he turned our lives, and the lives of everyone else in Iran, upside down and inside out.

Radical Moslems kept on organizing protests against the Shah, and in the end he imposed martial law. No one was allowed on the streets during the hours of darkness, but Iranian homes have flat roofs, and every night, for hours on end, the men would stand on their roofs and chant, "Death to the Shah! Death to America!" Lying in bed, listening to this chanting, was rather disconcerting.

The radical Moslems hated the movies made in Hollywood, because of their low moral standards. A cinema was set on fire while the audience was inside watching a movie – and many lives were lost. Also, close to our home, the Shah's forces massacred many protestors.

The foreign community tried to keep a low profile, but sometimes we had to go out to buy groceries. One time a group of Iranian youths challenged us, "Are you Americans?" When I said, "No, I am English and my wife is German," they said, "Then you are our friends," and they let us pass.

Because of all the disruptions to every-day life, some days the schools were open and other days they were not.

With the help of some young Iranian Christians, the boys were able to keep up with their lessons at the hostel.

Christmas 1978 was unforgettable. After the church service, we spent many hours feasting, giving gifts and playing games. In the end the boys were so exhausted they asked if they could go to bed!

Shortly after Christmas, we had to send them back to their homes, because it was getting too dangerous for them to be seen with us.

Then on January 16, 1979 the Shah and his family had to flee for their lives.

On February 1 Khomeini arrived in Iran after 15 years of exile.

And on February 8 the Bishop told me that he wanted me to go to England to take a course at a theological college.

I think he was trying to get us out of Iran before the revolution took place. We had three days to empty our lovely little house, and then Dimitri Bellos, who worked for the Bishop, was to drive us up to Tehran to catch a plane to London.

Marianne was very disappointed. She was seven months pregnant and really wanted our baby to be born in Iran. The English midwives at the hospital were our good friends.

Then on February 11, at six o'clock in the evening, when we were just locking up our now empty house, Dimitri came to tell us that the revolution had just started and we should go to the Bishop's house. We stayed five days with the Bishop and his very hospitable English wife, Margaret.

Then Dimitri, who, I think, was half Greek, half Russian, but had grown up in Iran, bravely drove us up to Tehran. A few times along the way we were stopped by groups of simple men and women, who had somehow acquired weapons, which they were proudly brandishing. When they saw Marianne was expecting, they let us go on.

We spent the night at the British Embassy in Tehran.

The next day, February 18, busloads of British people were transported to the airport. As we drove through the city, men and women shouted abuse at us. They didn't know how much we loved the country and people of Iran.

The British Royal Air Force was flying planeloads of people to Cyprus and then coming back for more. The seats in the plane were facing the wrong way, and the baby inside Marianne had hiccups four times on the trip.

In the end I felt so glad to leave. The Lord had brought us to Iran, where we had met each other, and now he was taking us away from there. The Lord had heard our prayers and the prayers of many others.

Some of our dear Iranian fellow-Christians were killed in the early days of the revolution.

And some of our friends, both Iranian and foreign, were imprisoned, including Dimitri. Eventually he and his Dutch wife, along with their family, were able to leave for the Netherlands.

THE GOD WHO ANSWERS PRAYER

Chapter Three

August 13, 2023

It took us 16 months to relocate from Esfahan, Iran to Cincinnati, Ohio. It was a very difficult time, but looking back, we can see God's loving hand in it all.

First, we crossed the island of Cyprus from the Royal Air Force base and caught a commercial flight to London, where the sister of a friend of ours had kindly offered to put us up for the night.

After spending some time with my family in Liverpool, we flew to Germany. Marianne's parents had plenty of room for us in their lovely home in the village of Martinsmoos in the Black Forest.

Marianne was expecting our first child. She developed high blood pressure and her doctor had her admitted into the hospital in Freudenstadt. Her due date was Easter Sunday, April 15, 1979.

Marianne's sister, Christa, drove Mama and me to visit her on Tuesday, April 10.

The original plan was that I should go home with them, but during the visit I had a strong feeling I should stay in Freudenstadt, and Mama kindly found me a room in a guest-house. I hardly knew any German and the lady didn't know any English. At three o'clock in the morning she received a call that I should go to the hospital and she woke me up.

It was a long and difficult labor because the baby was in the forehead-first position rather than the usual back-of-the-head-first position. She was finally born by vacuum ex-traction. It left a sore on her forehead, in which a staph infection developed.

So our dear Kathryn Silvia Spicer was born at 7:15 on Wednesday morning, April 11, 1979. I was thrilled to hold her while everyone was looking after Marianne.

Many years earlier I had gone to a Christian Holiday Home in Plas y Nant, Snowdonia, North Wales. A girl suddenly took hold of my hand, looked at the lines on it, and said, "You will never have any children." When Kathy was born, I felt that that curse was broken.

Because of the staph infection, Marianne and Kathy had to stay longer than usual in the hospital. Marianne was there for a total of 10 days.

On Easter Sunday morning I attended the beautiful Lutheran church on the town square. Although I didn't understand very much, I was happy to be with fellow Christians celebrating the resurrection of our Savior, the Lord Jesus Christ.

We were still hoping to go back to the Middle East, but Papa said, "No, that's too far away," even though, or perhaps because, he had spent 13 years in China, during which time the Second World War and the Chinese Communist Revolution had taken place.

Mama had heard of a German man in Berlin who wanted to share the gospel with Iranians. He had never been to Iran and didn't know any Persian, and wanted someone to help him. I went by train to visit him, passing through West Germany and what was then communist East Germany and into West Berlin through the infamous Berlin Wall.

The man had a very dominant personality, and I just knew it wouldn't work out.

During the time we had gone through martial law and the Islamic revolution in Iran, my shaking had worsened. Marianne's brother, Dr. Karl-Heinz Rink, who was working in Tübingen University Hospital at the time, got me admitted for tests free of charge. I spent six weeks in the hospital.

I was in a ward with five other men, none of whom spoke any English. Fortunately, I was allowed to go home at the weekends. My sister June, who worked in a bookstore in Liverpool, sent me quite a few books to keep me occupied, including Lady Antonia Fraser's hefty biographies of Mary, Queen of Scots and Oliver Cromwell, and Agatha Christie's auto-biography.

The doctors felt (wrongly as it later turned out) that I didn't have Parkinson's disease, but that I might have Wilson's disease, a rare condition caused by excess copper in the brain.

They asked me to go to England to see if the English doctors would confirm this or not. I spent three weeks in King's College Hospital in London. They tentatively agreed with Tübingen's diagnosis, even though my symptoms were not classic for Wilson's disease, and put me on Penicillamine to extract copper from my brain.

I applied for engineering jobs, but because I hadn't worked in that field for nine years, nobody wanted to employ me. When I applied for other jobs, they told me that I was over-qualified.

Every time I went for an interview, I prayed that if it was not the Lord's will for me to get that job, he would shut the door in my face, but every time it happened it was rather painful!

Christmas 1979 was spent in Germany with Marianne's family. Kathy was just eight months old and it was a very happy time. I had never seen such beautifully decorated Christmas trees, lit with real candles on the branches.

Meanwhile, the pastor of the Evangelical Fellowship Chapel in Cincinnati resigned. He asked if he could stay on until he found another church.

Marianne's godparents, Samuel & Luise Schulz, who had attended our wedding, had briefly been the pastor and pastor's wife of the church some ten years earlier. They suggested to Marianne's parents that we should go to Cincinnati. Papa was excited and called us in England. He said, "I have wonderful news for you! You're going to America!" I said, "But America is further away from Germany than the Middle East is." He said, "Yes, I know, but it's different." We thought, "Why should we go to America? There's a church on every street corner!" and quickly dismissed the whole idea.

Meanwhile, two ladies at the church in Cincinnati, who had heard about us from the Schulzens, met together regularly to pray that we would come, if that was the Lord's will.

Barry Kingdom, a fine Christian man who had founded a church in a poor neighborhood, heard about my need of employment and came to visit us. He told me that he knew a Christian man in the Ministry of Defence (British spelling!) who might be willing to give me a job.

The interview went well, but the man told me that I would have to design bombs and bullets. I knew, of course, that someone has to do that kind of work, but I wasn't sure that I should be the one.

I prayed that if this was not the Lord's will for me, it would not work out. I didn't hear from the man and felt relieved.

Then Barry came to see us again. He was amazed that I hadn't heard from his friend and said, "But he told me that he wants you for the job. I'll get in touch with him again."

Once more I prayed that if it was not the Lord's will, I wouldn't hear from the man, and I didn't.

I had also applied to a theological college, which trains pastors for the Baptist ministry. They sent me a book on church history, and told me (without ever meeting me) that if I passed a test based on that book, I would be accepted into their program.

But first Marianne and then I had a growing conviction that this was not the Lord's will for us. Finally, I mailed off a letter withdrawing my application. They were upset with me, saying that I should have talked it over with them first. However, decades later we heard that they promote doctrines which we believe are not Biblical. So the Lord spared us from going down a wrong path.

We began to feel there was no place for us in England. We decided we would visit Marianne's parents in Germany – we knew they would be happy to see us.

The day after we arrived, I began a job as a lathe operator, which someone had found for me. (As a teenager I had attended Wigan Technical College, and there I had learned to operate various machines.) It was a job I could do without having to speak German.

One day Papa told me that he wanted me to go to his home village in Hessen, about 180 miles north of Martinsmoos.

He wanted me to meet the Director of a group of churches in North America that had been founded to serve German immigrants, of which the church in Cincinnati was a part. The Director was visiting his father, with whom Papa had played when they were children.

I knew Papa was still hoping we would go to Cincinnati. I said to Marianne, "If Papa wants me to go and meet this man, I'll gladly go and meet him, but I know we will *not* go to America."

My brother-in-law, Siegfried, drove Mama and me up there, and I met the Director in his father's house. As we were talking, I felt the Lord was saying to me, "This is the way; walk in it." (Isaiah 30:21)

When we returned to Martinsmoos, I said to Marianne, "I think we're going to America." She was as stunned as I was!

On Saturday, May 10, 1980, Marianne's sister, Christa, married Hein Wubs from the Netherlands. They had met on OM Austria. They are a dear couple who live in the Black Forest surrounded by their many children and grandchildren.

The next day I flew to London to study a four-week-long course on teaching English to foreign students, which we had paid for earlier.

The school was in Piccadilly, right in the heart of everything. I loved being in a city so rich in history.

While I was in London, I stayed at the Honor Oak Christian Fellowship guest house, and attended the worship services there on Sundays.

Marianne in Germany and I in London were praying that the Lord would make it clear whether we should go to America or not, and on the same day we both felt that the Lord had shown us to go.

Bill Thompson of the Honor Oak Christian Fellowship had been the speaker at the OM conference in Tehran when we were granted Social Permission three years earlier.

One day I visited him at his home and said, "Neither of us particularly want to go to America, but we both feel that it's the Lord's will, so we are willing to go." He said, "That sounds like the Lord's will to me. If you had said, 'We've always wanted to go to America, and this is our golden opportunity,' I would have said, 'That doesn't sound like the Lord's will to me.'"

The Director had told us to come on tourist visas, and if the church people liked us and we wanted to stay, then I could apply for a work permit.

(This was all the wrong way of doing it, but none of us knew it at the time.)

I went to the American Embassy in London and asked for a tourist visa. They asked me, "Do you have a job in Britain to come back to?" to which I had to answer, "No." So they refused to give me a tourist visa.

When I told Marianne, she said, "Then we'll go to the American Consulate in Stuttgart, and if they give us a visa, that will be God's sign to me that he wants us to go. I don't want to take a 14-month-old child on such a long trip, just to see if the church people like us and we want to stay. I want God to give us his sign."

I very much wanted to see my family in Liverpool before going back to Germany, but didn't have enough money for the train tickets there and back.

I prayed for God's provision, but, much to my surprise, I felt the Lord was telling me to send £20 to a couple I knew in London. So I put the £20 note in an envelope and sent it to them anonymously, but the husband recognized my hand writing. He knew where I was staying and immediately wrote back, saying it had come at just the right moment for them.

Some dear Christian friends, nurses from Karlsruhe, with whom Marianne had once worked, visited her and gave her a gift of money, which she immediately mailed to me.

It arrived on the last day of the course, and I was able to exchange it for English money just before the bank closed. So I was able to visit my family in Liverpool, which turned out to be the last time I would see them for four years.

I flew back to Germany, and we went to the American Consulate in Stuttgart. The official told us to come back in two hours. We walked in the beautiful palace gardens in the warm sunshine, praying for God's will to be done. Much to our delight, they happily gave us our tourist visas.

On June 14, 1980 we flew to New York, and were driven the sixty miles to the denominational headquarters, where we attended the Pastors' Conference.

The denomination had originated in 1899 during a time of revival among house fellowship groups in East Prussia.

At some point, its churches in America and Canada had chosen to promote believers' baptism rather than infant baptism.

Each local congregation seemed to have a character of its own.

One of the pastors at the conference told me that there had been a quick succession of pastors in the Cincinnati Chapel, which was rather disconcerting. (I later learned that I was the 8th pastor in 10½ years.)

Then on June 24 we were driven to Cincinnati. Our sixteen months of wandering in the wilderness were over.

The former pastor had only just left, so we couldn't have come any earlier. The Lord knew what he was doing. Of course he did!

Praise the Lord, who led us so lovingly!

Amen.

Chapter Four

August 20, 2023

Charles Dickens begins *A Tale of Two Cities* with the words, "It was the best of times, it was the worst of times."

Life is a mixture of joys and sorrows, and this was particularly so during our first few years in Cincinnati.

Most, if not all, of the churches in our group were founded by German deaconesses. Sister Gertrude Harsch had founded the congregation in Cincinnati in 1961. Its first location was a house (1675 Chase Avenue in Northside).

However, in 1969 our headquarters made the decision that our churches should be led by male pastors and elders, rather than by the deaconesses.

Sister Gertrude told me that she had put out a sheet of paper and asked all who would like to become members of the church to sign it. There were no requirements for membership, such as being a born-again Christian.

She also put out another sheet of paper and asked all who wanted to become elders to sign it. Again, there were no requirements for eldership, such as being a born-again Christian.

The Director told the elders that they should provide health insurance for me and my family. He said to them, "Don't do to this pastor what you did to the last one." I was surprised he would say that in my presence.

The previous pastor had been very upset that they had not provided health insurance for him and his family. He confided in Bob Cload, who was a member of another church, and Bob tried to help him in every way he could.

As soon as Bob heard of my arrival, he came to meet me and assure me of his help. As we talked, I found out that he had spent a summer in Italy with Operation Mobilization, and that he had also lived in Liverpool for a year, helping out in a ministry there. So we had plenty in common, and he was a great blessing to me, especially in those early years.

When we went to the immigration office, we were told that we had done everything the wrong way. The official told me that I could work as the pastor, but that I couldn't receive any salary.

Sister Gertrude asked if the church could give me a gift. He replied, "Not more than $50 a week."

I think our case was deliberately slow-walked to teach us a lesson. It took more than three years to resolve it. Our time with OM was good training for living on $50 a week.

When we first arrived, the parsonage had hardly any furniture in it. There were two single beds in one bedroom, and a crib in another. We were grateful that one couple had lent us a loveseat for the living room, and another couple had lent us an oval table and some chairs for the dining room.

I had only brought one book with me – a pocket-sized Bible from which I preached.

That first summer, Marianne's sister, Christa, and her husband, Hein, came to see us. Hein told us that he wanted to wallpaper our bedroom for us. Although he was legally blind, he did a great job. The wallpaper was really lovely and we enjoyed it for many years.

We kept saying, "When we finally get our salary, we'll buy such-and-such for the house," but we had said it about so many different things that it took years to buy them all.

We were invited to the homes of the church families for meals, especially at the holidays, which we really enjoyed.

Iran had been much hotter, but it was a dry heat. That first summer Marianne was overwhelmed by the humidity, but she got used to it over the next few years.

At the first elders' meeting, one of the elders told me they would *not* provide health insurance for us, but if we needed any medical attention they would pay for it.

He also told me that as long as he was an elder, our debt to our headquarters would not be paid back.

In 1969 the headquarters had lent the congregation $75,000 to buy the property, including the house on it, and to buy all the materials to build the church.

Sister Gertrude explained to me that one time she wasn't able to pay the electric bill and asked the elders what she should do. This elder (who was very rich) told her to ask our headquarters to pay the bill. They rightly refused, and he said, "Then we won't pay back our debt to them." I thought of Psalm 37:21 – "The wicked borrow and do not repay."

I asked Sister Gertrude if she would go over the membership list with me and tell me which ones she felt were born-again Christians. She felt that only about one-third of them were.

Poor Sister Gertrude couldn't sleep, worrying about how to pay the bills.

Some of the women would threaten to withhold their offerings if she didn't do what they wanted her to do.

She took me to the homes of many German people who were not a part of our congregation. I noticed that these people would usually give her a gift for the church. I think that without those gifts she couldn't have paid the bills.

One day I received a phone call from an elderly woman who occasionally came to the church. She told me that her son-in-law was dying, and asked me to go to the hospital and pray for him. I didn't have my driver's license yet, so she told me she would send her granddaughter to pick me up. While I was waiting, I knelt by my bed and asked the Lord to guide me. I felt he was saying to me, "Just pray a simple prayer of faith and I will heal him."

When we arrived at the hospital, a young doctor was explaining to the family that the man's blood had become toxic and had affected all his organs, and that he only had about 24 hours to live. I waited for the doctor to leave, and said to the family, "Don't worry; we'll pray for him and he will be healed." And he was. This was the only time in my life I experienced anything like this.

However, when I went to visit him a day or two later, he didn't want to have anything to do with me.

The church bought us a 9-seater 1975 Buick Station Wagon for $700. It was more than 19 feet long (almost 6 meters)! Four years earlier, Marianne had helped drive a van from Germany to Iran, but she refused to drive this "monster," as she called it. Later she did drive it when I couldn't anymore.

Eventually, the church did pay for our health insurance. At that time it cost $80 per month.

Marianne's parents came to visit us for two months in the spring of 1981. They loved America.

When they returned home, they sent us enough money to buy furniture for our living room, dining room and bedroom. We still have quite a lot of it.

In the fall of 1981, my brother, Doug, came for the first of fourteen visits to us – basically, once a year until his early death from cancer. We were all very close to him.

Mrs. Plokarz was moving to Chicago and gave us her piano, which we still have. Later on our house was full of music as our children practiced their pieces on it.

I would call Mrs. Zilian and ask her to pray for me. I never told her any details or what to pray for. One time I said to her, "Did you pray for me?" She said, "You better believe it. As soon as I hung up the phone, I got down on my knees, and prayed for you for two hours." At a very dark time in our lives, she was the only one who gave me a word of encouragement. Her English was cute. She called intensive care "expensive care," and Alzheimer's disease "old timer's disease." Like many of the other women, she called pneumonia "ammonia." Her death in a road accident was a great loss to me and to all of us.

The first indication that something had gone wrong in my body happened while the youth group was playing baseball. I swung the bat over my shoulder, but my body "froze" and I couldn't move my arms forward. None of us understood what was happening.

Marianne was expecting our second child, and when premature labor began at 30 weeks, she was told she had to rest. Some of the women, especially Sister Gertrude and Brigitta Hetzel, who lived close by, came and helped wherever they could.

Finally the right time had come and I drove Marianne to the hospital. Our precious Stephanie Anna Spicer was born at 7:21 a.m. on Tuesday, November 3, 1981.

I was born in England, Marianne in China, Kathy in Germany and now we had our first American baby. 3 more American babies would follow in due time.

While Marianne was in labor, I was experiencing a different kind of great pain. At the time we didn't realize what was going on. The Penicillamine was supposed to be removing copper from my brain, but, was, in fact, demineralizing my whole body.

Without realizing the damage I was doing, I kept taking the medication for another year, and so my bones were getting weaker and weaker.

In late June 1982 I drove the family up to our denominational headquarters. I had never driven such a long distance before (625 miles). My body was totally broken down.

While we were there, we received the sad news that Marianne's father had died. He was 74. We were so sorry to lose him. We loved him very much. Marianne couldn't go to the funeral in Germany because we were not yet properly immigrated into America, but Ilse & Siegfried, and their 17-month-old son, Nikolaj (pronounced *Nikolai*), came to join us at the headquarters.

I had to fly home, and Siegfried drove the station wagon with everyone in it back to Cincinnati.

The muscles in my abdomen were as stiff as a board. It took me half an hour to get into bed and half an hour to get out again. I couldn't turn over in bed without Marianne's help.

We didn't realize it at the time, but Stephanie was allergic to mothers' milk. She cried a lot, and Marianne had to get up many times each night to see to Stephanie and to help me. I don't remember Marianne ever complaining. When Stephanie was weaned at 16 months, she started to sleep better.

My spine collapsed and I lost 5½ inches in height within a short time. The shortening of my spine put strain on my breastbone and one day it snapped. Later on it healed in an overlapped way.

Marianne bought me a recliner because I couldn't get in and out of bed anymore.

My neurologist suggested that I should go to the Mayo Clinic, where he had once worked. We were there for the whole month of November 1982. One of the ladies in the church very kindly paid for our motel room.

The Mayo Clinic is in the small town of Rochester, Minnesota. At that time there were just five fast-food restaurants in the town, but no better places to eat. We celebrated Stephanie's first birthday in one of those fast-food restaurants.

Dr. Campbell was in charge of my case. He was from Birkenhead, across the river from Liverpool, just as Covington is across the river from Cincinnati.

He asked me, "Did you come to America for better pay?" I explained that we were not yet immigrated, and that the church was not allowed to give me more than $50 a week. He must have told the other doctors not to charge me anything, but we didn't know that until the end of the month.

He immediately took me off the Penicillamine and told me, "If you don't lose any more height, then you can know it was the Penicillamine that did it to you."

However, he added, "That's just between you and me. I will not testify for you if you decide to sue your doctor."

He looked at my test results from Germany and England, and said that no one in America would regard those copper levels as elevated.

He told me that I didn't have Wilson's disease, but that I did have Parkinson's disease after all.

He prescribed the standard medication for Parkinson's disease, Carbidopa-Levidopa, and as soon as I took the first tablet, my shaking stopped. It was such a relief. I had struggled with shaking on and off for almost a quarter of a century.

Another doctor there told me that my bone density was at the 5th percentile, which meant that 95% of people had higher bone density than I did and 5% had lower. He told me, "Within seven years you will be confined to a wheelchair for the rest of your life." He was operating on the assumption that my bone density would continue to decline.

I just prayed silently, "Lord, how do you want me to deal with this?" and I felt the Lord say, "Just ignore it," which I did, and by God's grace, I never worried about it.

More than forty years have passed by since then, and his prediction has not proved true. (As soon as I came off the Penicillamine my bone density began to rebound.)

On Thanksgiving Day all the fast-food restaurants in Rochester were closed. I told the receptionist at the motel, and he said, "I'll make you some cheese sandwiches." We will never forget his kindness.

The total cost for the month at the Mayo Clinic was a little over a thousand dollars. The health insurance paid most of it and the church paid the remaining $365.

That one elder told me I should sue the doctors in Germany and England. He said, "You could get a million dollars!" But I felt that the Lord wouldn't want me to do that. They hadn't deliberately harmed me. They had made a mistake, but there was no malicious intent. (Also, I couldn't have left America because I wasn't properly immigrated yet.)

Twelve months later we went back to the Mayo Clinic for a checkup. They took X-rays and told me that I'd had about three dozen fractures of the ribcage, which had since healed. This explains why I had been in so much pain.

Later, I was suddenly stricken with arthritis in my hips and knees. When I asked an arthritis specialist what he could do for me, all he could say was, "Well, not much. All we can do is give you pain medication."

Shortly after this I came across the book, "There *is* a Cure for Arthritis" by Paavo Airola ND, originally published in 1968 and still available.

He described health clinics in Sweden and Germany which treated arthritis patients by putting them on a juice fast for 10 to 17 days. This was to cleanse out their bodies. The results were remarkable. Many were completely cured, even those who had arrived on crutches or in wheelchairs.

I went to see Dr. Neil Aldridge, a naturopathic doctor I knew, and asked him if he had ever read the book. He said, "No, but I've read other books by him, and I've read other books on the subject. If you follow my instructions, you will only have to juice fast for 6 days and you will be free of your arthritis."

He gave me a list of six different juices. Each day, instead of eating food and drinking caffeinated drinks, I was to drink a gallon of one particular freshly-made juice.

Unfortunately, I didn't keep the list, but I remember that one day I drank a gallon of celery juice and another day a gallon of pineapple juice. On the last day I was to drink beet (or beetroot) juice. The doctor said I would be lucky to drink a pint of it, and, in fact, I only managed a third of a pint, but by the end of the sixth day the arthritis was gone. It was certainly worth it. That was about 40 years ago, and it has never come back. All praise to God! I doubt that I would still be alive if I had not done it. (Also, it's not as difficult as many people imagine.)

One Wednesday in May 1983, we received a letter from the immigration office saying that we had to leave the country within two weeks. Later that day, I read a very inspiring magazine article about trusting God. When the people came for the mid-week meeting, I read the article to them and then we prayed. That evening and early the next morning four different people suggested that we should go to see Guy Guckenberger, a Cincinnati City Council member and immigration lawyer. So Sister Gertrude, Marianne and I went to see him. He sprang into action, and within a short time everything was sorted out and we had our "green cards," which, incidentally, are not green but white and blue.

During those years, there were other challenges which were far more difficult than the physical ones, great as they were. We praise the Lord that he carried us through them all.

We only rarely had guest speakers, but at a very difficult time, the Lord sent us eight guest speakers in an eleven week period, which was very encouraging to me.

On January 25, 1984, the Director drove Sister Gertrude back to the headquarters.

As their car was going down the driveway, I prayed that the Lord would give Sister Gertrude ten years of fruitful service at the headquarters.

On January 25, 1994, I said to Marianne, "Sister Gertrude left us ten years ago today." That evening we received a call telling us that Sister Gertrude had had a heart attack and had been hospitalized. A few days later, she had a second heart attack and died.

So God answered that prayer to the very day. It is statistically impossible for this to be a coincidence. Our God answers prayers in ways far beyond our understanding.

Marianne says, "He is totally trustworthy and entirely dependable." And he is! Of course he is!

Praise our great God forever! Amen.

THE GOD WHO ANSWERS PRAYER

Chapter Five

August 27, 2023

In April 1984 Kathy turned five and needed to be registered in a kindergarten. The closest school had a good reputation and we thought she would be able to go there, like her friends who lived just a few houses away from us on the street behind the church property. However, we were told that she had to go to another school which was further away. When we went to register her, we didn't come away with a good impression of the school. We knew someone who worked at the Board of Education, so I called to ask her what she thought of the school. She said, "It's the worst school in the district and the principal's a clown." So we began to pray that God would show us what to do.

We considered a certain Christian school, but their kindergarten program was eight hours a day, including a two-hour nap. This didn't sound right to us. Also, it was very expensive.

Then Marianne read an article about home schooling. We had never heard of such a thing. Then someone else recommended it to us.

Finally, we attended a Greg Harris home school conference in Wilmington, Ohio with our friends, Bob and Ruth Cload. Marianne and I decided to home school Kathy beginning in September. We ordered a curriculum from Christian Liberty Academy in Chicago, which we were very pleased with.

At that time, most of the pastors in our denomination were from Germany. Every four years our headquarters paid half of the flights for our pastors and their families to go back for a visit. This was very generous of them, and without their help we couldn't have gone. Mama kindly offered to pay the other half.

Our original plan was to go to the 1984 Pastors' Conference at our headquarters, then spend two weeks with my family in England, and finally go on to Germany.

Our friend, Anni Kane, who lived close to the headquarters, found out that we would be flying to England on the same night that she and her family would be flying to Germany, and she suggested that we should all travel to the airport in New York City together.

Then Mama asked us if we would be willing to change our flight to July 4, which would be cheaper for her.

This would mean spending five extra days at the headquarters and five days less with my family in England. I told her we would call her back in an hour. We prayed about it and I felt we should honor her as the only parent we still had, especially as she was paying for us.

As Anni and her family were being driven to the airport by some friends, the station wagon they were in was suddenly engulfed in flames and they lost everything except their lives. We would have been with them. We were so grateful that the Lord protected us in this remarkable way.

I had been taking the Parkinson's medication for more than one and a half years. It stopped the shaking, which was an immense relief to me. However, I had 23 of the 48 side effects listed.

While we were in Germany, Marianne asked me if I would be willing to stop taking the medication and just put up with the shaking. She didn't want me to have to deal with the side effects, some of which were quite distressing. I told her I would pray about it.

I returned to America alone, and Marianne and the children stayed with Mama for a few more weeks.

The smaller house on the church property was empty at that time.

For 4½ days I slept in the bigger house each night, but spent each day in the smaller house because it didn't have a phone. I waited on the Lord and felt that he wanted me to do what Marianne had suggested. So for fifteen years (1984-1999) I didn't take the medication, and my family and the congregation kindly bore with my continual shaking and decline.

Our Director asked all the pastors in our group to preach on what the Bible teaches about abortion, pornography and other issues.

I had just read an excellent slim volume, *Secular Humanism* by Homer Duncan, and decided to summarize it as an introduction to the other sermons. I closed the message with, "Next week I will speak on abortion."

If I had anticipated any negative reaction, I would have explained that our Director had asked all of our pastors to speak on this and the other subjects, but I naively presumed that all Christians would be against abortion.

After the service one of the women said to me, "I've talked it over with the other women, and if you speak on abortion next week, there are seven of us who will leave the church."

I prayed about it and felt I should not give in to their empty threats, and none of them left, at least not at that time.

At the end of the sermon on abortion I didn't say, "Next week I will speak on pornography." I was learning my lessons.

A woman and her daughter both had husbands, who, unknown to me, were deeply involved in pornography. The women were always trying to get their husbands to come to church, and that week both men agreed to come.

I must have said, "I believe" such-and-such, and the younger husband said to me, "We don't come to church to hear what you believe; we come to hear what the Bible says," and, of course, he was right, and that was another lesson learned.

The older woman complained, "The one time we get our husbands to come to church, you speak on pornography!"

At 2:15 in the afternoon on Wednesday, July 31, 1985 our lovely daughter, Amy Elisabeth Spicer, was born in our home.

Our children and some of their friends, a few of the church people and two German girls who had come over to help us crowded in to see the new-born baby. It was quite an event, and the midwives were concerned about all the visitors.

In September 1986, a man I had never met before came to see me. He knew some of the people in our congregation and said, "There's sin in your church, and you're not doing anything about it." From what Sister Gertrude had shared with me and from what I knew myself, I knew he was speaking the truth.

For the next two months I spent time every day asking the Lord what I should do. I tried to speak with the people involved, but they refused to speak with me. A church business meeting was scheduled for the end of November, and as we really didn't have anything else more pressing to discuss, I decided to use that occasion to challenge the people to turn from their sins. At first there was a good response, but then someone changed the subject and all hell broke loose.

Apparently, a number of the women called the Director and demanded that he should immediately come down to Cincinnati and throw me out.

The people had built the church building with their own hands, which was a remarkable achievement, and it was understandable that they felt a great sense of ownership.

I prayed, "Lord, if you want me to resign, I am totally willing to do so," but I felt him say, "No, if you resign, then the next pastor will have to go through everything you've had to go through."

We lived in great tension for the next twelve months, during which time Marianne twice lost a baby at four months.

I remember a few things from that year:

The Director didn't come for four months, and when he finally came, the women refused to meet with him. Other people, though, were happy to speak with him.

One woman sat on the front pew week after week, glaring at me as I preached. She left through the side door so that she wouldn't have to shake hands with me. We tried to visit her, but she shut the door in our faces. However, someone told me that she had said, "I can't deny that he preaches the truth."

Another woman told the elders that she wanted to speak to them about Marianne and me. One of the elders said, "Only if Brian and Marianne are there too."

For two hours straight she falsely accused us and misrepresented what we had said and done. We couldn't believe our ears. Later I read in 1 Timothy 5:22, "Do not entertain an accusation against an elder [or pastor] unless it is brought by two or three witnesses."

One Sunday, just as the worship service was about to begin, I felt I couldn't go through with the meeting. I went downstairs to pray in the storage room. I felt the Lord say to me, "Look to me and be radiant!" I said, "Lord, I look to you. Please make me radiant!" After the service one of the women who were against me said, "Brian, you were radiant today!" I didn't know she was familiar with that word.

One day one of our ladies said to me, "I think you should know that such-and-such a woman said to me, 'Don't put anything in the offering. Then there won't be enough money to pay Brian, and he'll have to leave. Then we'll get a pastor who'll do what we want him to do.'"

A number of the women refused to come to the church as long as I was there.

On July 28, 1987, Marianne's sister, Ilse, found her three-month-old son, Benjamin, dead in his crib.

Marianne went to Germany to spend some time with her, taking along two-year-old Amy.

The elders told me that the women wanted a vote whether I should remain the pastor or not. I prayed quietly, "Lord, how do you want me to handle this?" I felt him say, "Let them have their vote."

Then one of the elders said, "This is a list of those who are allowed to vote." When I looked at it, I saw the names of people who hadn't attended the church during the seven years I had been the pastor. When I pointed this out, he said, "They came to the Sunday School when they were young, so they have the right to determine the future of the church." Also, the names of others who faithfully attended the church were not on the list. When I pointed this out, he said, "No, they are not allowed to vote." Again, I prayed quietly, "Lord, how do you want me to handle this?" I felt him say, "Let them have their list."

The Director was away on a two-month-long trip to the Far East, visiting mission stations that our churches helped to support. So the date of the vote was set for Sunday, November 8.

I said to Marianne, "Let's go away for ten days."

So at the end of September, we and our three young daughters were just about to drive off to *cleftRock*, a Christian retreat center in Kentucky, when Bob Cload suddenly appeared to give me a book he wanted me to read while we were away. It was *This Present Darkness* by Frank Peretti. It was a novel, but almost certainly based on an actual situation. Marianne had already read it.

In the book, the pastor, Hank Busch, spoke out about sin in the church, and the congregation demanded a vote whether he should remain the pastor or not. 28 voted for him to stay, and 26 voted for him to leave.

I prayed, "Lord, if you would do that for me, then I would know that *you* want me to stay at the church." At that time, all I meant was that if the vote would go in my favor, even by the slimmest of margins, then I would know that the Lord wanted me to stay at the church.

The Director came to conduct the vote. While we were all down at the church, five faithful friends were in our living room praying for us.

The vote was supposed to take place at 7:00 p.m.

However, one woman had gone to the airport to pick up her daughter, and everyone else's luggage was there, but her daughter's was not. So they called the church to ask if the vote could be put back half an hour to give them a chance to find it. Everyone agreed and sat in stony silence for half an hour. (The mother and daughter never turned up.)

The Director said to me, "The women think that they only need a simple majority, but, strictly speaking, the constitutions of all the churches in our denomination say that a vote of 75% is required to call a pastor and a vote of 85% is required to dismiss a pastor. 54 people are present, so, strictly speaking, they would need 46 votes to dismiss you."

He also said that all the constitutions of our churches say that if anyone of their own free will has not attended the church for six months they forfeit their church membership, which, strictly speaking, would apply to some of these women, disqualifying them from the right to vote.

Finally one of the elders said, "We can't wait any longer. Let's have the vote."

When the votes had been counted, he announced, "28 have voted for the pastor to stay." I turned to Marianne and said, "Hank Busch." She nodded.

I just knew that he would say, "and 26 have voted for the pastor to leave," and he did!

Those who lost the vote immediately stood up and left. They never came back, except for funerals, just as it had been in the book.

The following Sunday only 38 attended the worship service. 76 had attended the week before. A young man who had grown up in the church said to me, "Don't be discouraged. This was the first time I ever felt freedom in my spirit to worship the Lord."

We prayed that those who left us would find good churches, and many of them did. Our paths have crossed many times throughout the years, especially at funerals.

This was an amazing answer to prayer. Again, it is statistically impossible for this to be a coincidence.

Praise Almighty God, the God of the universe, who answers the prayers of his servants, unworthy as they are.

Amen.

THE GOD WHO ANSWERS PRAYER

Chapter Six

September 3, 2023

The following events took place between 1988 and 1999:

On September 30, 1988 Mama called to tell us that she had cancer. We had been with her in the summer, and she had served us wholeheartedly, as she always did. Neither she nor we suspected anything, but when we looked back at the photos we'd taken, we could see that she hadn't looked so well.

In October she had an operation, and then Marianne flew alone to Germany to help her for the whole month of November.

Then in April 1989 Marianne went over again for another four weeks, during which time her beloved mother died. She was 76. Günther & Edith Pareigis and Joe Willhite from our church were in Germany at that time and visited Marianne, which was a great encouragement to her.

The first Sunday after Mama's death, while Marianne was still in Germany, we held a memorial service in our church, because everyone knew and loved her.

She had visited us for a total of eleven months over the years. Whenever she was with us, she played the organ in our church, which she dubbed "the whimpering organ," because she was used to playing a real pipe organ in Germany. I remember saying that she was the greatest Christian I had ever met, which not many people can say about their mother-in-law.

We were expecting again. Because Marianne had safely delivered three girls, and had miscarried four boys, the doctor told her that she probably would never have a boy. When she returned from Germany, she was already seven months along, so we presumed she was carrying a girl. The midwives felt that, because of the grief of losing her mother, she should have an ultrasound to see how the baby was doing.

They were not allowed to tell us whether the baby was a boy or a girl unless we asked, and we didn't ask. They knew us and our history, so they said, "Don't you want to know whether it's a *boy* or a girl?" Marianne said, "Oh, we know it's a girl," and then they told us it was a boy. We laughed all the way home. It took us a couple of weeks to get used to the idea! Marianne had fun buying little clothes for a baby boy.

Our son's due date was Thursday, July 13, but I was supposed to be in Oklahoma City at that time. We prayed he would come ten days early so I could be at his birth and help Marianne afterwards. We prayed that he wouldn't come at the weekend, always our busiest time, and that Marianne would have a full night's sleep Sunday to Monday, and that all the labor would take place during the daylight hours on Monday, July 3, and that's exactly what the Lord did for us!

At seven o'clock in the evening of July 3, 1989 our beloved son, Timothy Brian Spicer, was born in Bethesda Hospital on Oak Street in Cincinnati, exactly ten weeks after his grandmother's death.. We were so awed that God had answered all the details of our prayers.

We were getting older, but still hoping and praying that God would give us another child. When we found out we were expecting again, we were so grateful that God had heard our prayers.

When Marianne was five months along, I had some water removed from my knee. Then Marianne asked the doctor if he could X-ray my back. He told me I would end up being paralyzed from the chest down, and even described my death in great detail.

It was all very disconcerting. What would happen to my wife and five children? I didn't sleep for three days and nights, but then I read these reassuring words: "Because he loves me," says the Lord, "I will rescue him; I will protect him, for he acknowledges my name. He will call upon me, and I will answer him; I will be with him in trouble, I will deliver him and honor him. With *long life* will I satisfy him and show him my salvation" (Psalm 91:14-16). All my fears evaporated and I didn't worry about it anymore. More than thirty years have passed by since then, and I praise the Lord that the doctor's grim predictions didn't take place.

Twenty months after Tim's birth, our bundle of joy, Emily Joy Spicer, was born at home on Thursday, March 7, 1991, at 2:15 a.m., making our family complete. All her siblings were thrilled to hold her and coo over her.

We knew that during the summer of 1992, we would be in England and Germany for a total of six weeks, and were praying that someone would stay at our house to look after our many pets and plants. The Lord answered in a very amazing way:

A young couple, Jon & Robin Vermilion, were joining the staff of *Campus Crusade for Christ* in Wake Forest, North Carolina.

Because they had both had some connection with Cincinnati in the past, *Campus Crusade* asked them to raise support in our city.

Jon called a church on the other side of Cincinnati, and the pastor's wife gave him a list of churches he could call. Ours was the first on the list, which was rather surprising as we hardly knew her. Jon explained to me that they needed a place to stay in Cincinnati at such-and-such a time – the exact dates we would be away! It gave me great pleasure to tell him that they could stay at our house.

We first spent three weeks at a guest house in Southport, a seaside resort 20 miles north of Liverpool. My sister June and her sons, John and Paul; then my sister Audrey and her husband, George, and their dogs; and finally my brother Doug each spent one week at the hotel with us. I was so happy my sisters could meet 3-year-old Tim and 16-month-old Emily for the first time.

We noticed June had slowed down a lot, and just four months later, on November 16, 1992, she had a brain aneurism and died later that same day. She was 62. When I returned to England for her funeral, I realized we had never had a cross word in the 46 years we had been brother and sister.

Ian and Norma Macdougal, an English couple who attended the church, told us they might move back to England, and asked us, if they did, whether we would buy their brown Astro van for $2,000, to which we happily agreed. They did decide to go back, and as Ian was driving the van to us, a tire blew and instead of buying one new tire he bought four. I tried very hard to pay him for the new tires, but he absolutely wouldn't hear of it.

In the fall of 1995, my brother Doug was diagnosed with cancer and operated on.

In January 1996 I visited him at his home in Rainhill, close to Liverpool. I expected him to be very weak, but he was eager to do things and go places. We flew the 90 miles to the Isle of Man, an island in the middle of the Irish Sea, where our mother was born and spent the first thirteen years of her life. Our cousin, May Holmes, drove us all around the beautiful island.

Marianne, the children and I were planning to visit England and Germany in the summer, so I was looking for a hotel on Mount Pleasant in downtown Liverpool where we could stay.

Joan and Peter Smith had come up from Northampton to stay with Stan and Eileen Bulman, who were old friends of mine too.

(Joan was the one who had challenged me to go on the Project Evangelism outreach 26 years earlier, thus changing the whole direction of my life.)

They invited me over for an evening, and Stan asked me, "Where will you stay in the summer?" I said, "Well, I've been looking at hotels on Mount Pleasant." He said, "Don't stay on Mount Pleasant! You can stay in our home, and while you're here, we'll go away on our holidays." That was so kind of them. What a wonderful provision!

Also, Erika Mauer, a dear old friend from Iptingen, Germany, the village where Marianne grew up, invited us to stay with her for a week.

The Lord was looking after us through these wonderful friends.

Before we went to Europe, Doug paid us one last visit in May 1996. It was very sad to see him looking so weak and tired, lying on the sofa much of the time. For the last full day of his vacation, we decided to go to Lake Kincaid in Kentucky. We were almost there when a woman, who should have stopped at a stop sign, drove straight into us. I could see her coming and made a loud cry, which helped the others to brace themselves.

Everyone at the scene of the accident was very kind to us, and our friend, Mark Hetzel, drove the 35 miles to pick us all up.

Marianne's sternum was cracked in two places. The insurance paid for her medical bills and gave us $1,800 for pain and suffering. Our vehicle was totaled. They gave us $4,400, which was a lot more than the $2,000 we had paid for it. The two amounts came to $6,200. Earlier we had paid our headquarters our part towards our upcoming trip to Europe, but they had just told us that we had to pay some more. Also, we were slowly paying off medical bills for Kathy and Emily at so much per week. We paid off all the bills, and that left us with exactly $4,000.

We were praying that God would provide a van for that amount so that we could go to our headquarters in June. Someone expressed doubt that God would give us another van, which only made us pray all the more.

Four days before we had to leave for our headquarters, Mark Hetzel mentioned that he had seen an Astro van for $3,900 in a used car lot. The next day we went with Mark to have a look at it. We liked it, but it needed a few repairs, including the air conditioning, which the man willingly did for us.

I asked if the price plus the sales tax (5% at that time) could come to $4,000, because that was all we had, and he quite happily agreed to that too. His wife was a notary public and saw to all the paperwork. When we arrived home with the van, we all held hands and praised the Lord for his wonderful provision.

Marianne's father had been the Lutheran pastor of Iptingen (1954-65) when Marianne was 3-14 years old. (She was born on October 1, 1950). The ladies of the village who remembered her and her family put on a wonderful *Backhausfest* for us. They fired up the centuries-old communal baking oven in the center of the village, and baked pizzas, quiches, and German specialties such as onion pies and oil cakes. While we were eating, bread was baking in the oven. It all brought back so many happy memories to Marianne. We noticed a great openness to the gospel. One family we spoke to invited us to their home the following evening so that they could ask us more questions. They later wrote to us that they had "said yes to Jesus," a German way of expressing themselves.

The week before we arrived there, a German Christian group had held a Tent Mission in Iptingen.

No doubt people all over Germany were praying for openness in the village. They were the most open people we have ever met. This shows the great power of prayer.

I was with my brother Doug when he died on January 19, 1997. He was 49. Marianne arrived a couple of hours later and was a great support to me. We were there together for his funeral.

I found it very hard to get over his death. He was 15 months younger, but built bigger, than I was, and the neighbors referred to us as "Mrs. Spicer's twins." He was my closest sibling, not only in age. We had a photo of him in our bedroom, which was the first thing I saw every morning. When I looked at it, I felt like a dagger was going through my heart. After about a year of this I took the photo down and put it in a drawer, and slowly began to recover.

When Kathy graduated from home school/high school, I asked her if there was anything she would like to do. She told me she was interested in doing an intensive course in Russian language and culture in Indianapolis, and then serving in a Christian orphanage in Moscow.

We had been struggling financially for many months.

One day I prayed, "Lord, we need an infusion of $400. Would you please provide it from the least likely source?" A few days later an envelope arrived with a check for $400 in it. It was from Mike Litteral, a man who lived among the Amish in Ohio, although he himself was not Amish. Our paths had crossed a couple of times, but we didn't know each other that well. When I called to thank him, he was not home, but his wife told me he'd had the strongest compulsion to send me $400.

When Marianne was in seventh and eighth grades, she made friends with her biology teacher, Fräulein Christa Lemppenau, and they stayed in touch for over forty years until her teacher's death. In 1997 she sent us a large gift of money for music lessons and other school needs.

Kathy did very well in the Russian course, and we were praying that the Lord would provide the funds for her to go to Russia. Marianne raised $600 with a yard sale. Kerry and Barbara Staller bought her a warm coat and boots, and our neighbor, Mrs. Vockell, and Fräulein Lemppenau gave large gifts. Praise God! He made it very clear that Kathy should go. She worked at the orphanage in Moscow from December 1997 till May 1998.

In 1998 our dear friend, Bill Glasgow, totally surprised us by giving us his green 1994 Dodge Caravan XL with 97,000 miles on it. We drove it for another 100,000 miles and passed it on with 197,000 miles on it to someone who drove it for many thousands of miles before passing it on to yet someone else. What a blessing!

The Lord provided the funds for three very special trips in 1999:

In the spring, I read a letter from *Open Doors with Brother Andrew* describing an upcoming trip to China to bring in Bibles, Christian books and videos in tribal languages, and I had a strong feeling that Marianne should be a part of it. She had left China in 1951 when she was only 10 months old.

A later letter from *Open Doors* shared the itinerary. It included Kunming (where Marianne's brother, Karl-Heinz, was born) and Dali (where Marianne was born), both in Yünnan province in SW China. Then I felt even more strongly that she should go, and she did.

In Dali two elderly people, who had worked at the mission hospital at the time of Marianne's birth, showed her the delivery room, the very place where she had been born!

The building was in a rather dilapidated condition due to a badly damaged roof and was scheduled to be demolished within two years.

Open Doors was also sending a team to help the persecuted Christians in Chiapas, the southernmost state of Mexico, bordering on Guatemala, and Stephanie very much wanted to go. However, because she was only 17½, and not yet 18, they told her she couldn't go. I called their headquarters in California, but they said there was *no way* she could be on the team. When I told Stephanie, she said, "Dad, I know I'll be on that team." She didn't waver, and one day they called her to say she could join them. After she returned, a few members of the team called me to say what a great blessing she had been.

My nephew, Paul Vernon, told me he was going to marry an Irish girl, Ethna Roddy, in Belfast, Northern Ireland. He asked me if I would preach his wedding sermon. By this time I was in a very pitiful state with my Parkinson's disease. I rarely went out during the daylight hours because I was often unable to take the next step. After dark I would take our beagle, Copper, for a walk around the block. If I "froze," he would wait patiently until I was able to start walking again.

I realized it was now time for me to see a neurologist again. He told me it was good that I hadn't taken the medicine for the previous fifteen years, because it can lose its effectiveness over time, but that it was now time for me to take it again. I was very reluctant, because this was the medicine that had caused me so much distress, but it's really the only medicine that works for Parkinson's. He assured me it had been improved and was now controlled-release. As soon as I took it, my shaking stopped, and I could walk freely again without "freezing."

As we landed in Belfast, the pilot told us that it was 58 degrees Fahrenheit (14 degrees Celsius). I thought, "Well, I guess that's not too bad," but when Paul and his best man met us, they were ecstatic, saying, "This is the *hottest* it's been all summer." We were there for two weeks and the high temperatures ranged between 58 and 60. Everyone kept telling us how lucky we were to have such *hot* weather.

Paul had found a cottage for us to stay in, and said that we could attend the large, modern Methodist church close by. However, as we were walking to the shore, we saw a sign outside a less impressive building.

In gold letters on a black background, it said, "The word of the Lord is preached here every Lord's Day at 4:00 p.m." For some reason I felt we should go there.

We had spent some time on the rocky shore before going to the church. We were totally windswept. Our hair was all over the place and we didn't have a comb. A young man, Nigel Lyons, was standing outside and invited us in.

There were seven people inside, including Nigel, and the seven of us doubled the congregation. They sang without any musical accompaniment.

Nigel's brother, Jeremy, gave a very powerful presentation of the gospel. It was excellent. Then they invited us to the Sunday morning service the next week, and we walked the short distance to our cottage. I said, "Let's just have a bowl of cereal and go back to the shore." Suddenly Nigel was at the door, inviting us to eat with him and his wife. I said, "Oh, we've just eaten some cereal." He said, "Oh, that's nothing," and urged us to come. We had a few hours of very sweet fellowship with them. We had definitely gone to the right place. I asked them if I could use the church building to prepare the wedding sermon, and they very readily agreed.

One highlight of our trip to Ireland was going to Newcastle, County Down, where, as the song says, the Mountains of Mourne "sweep down to the sea." It was such a joy for me to climb half way up *Slieve Donard* and sit for a long time on a ledge overlooking the Irish Sea. I had happy memories of climbing it when I was a young teenager. A couple of weeks earlier I could hardly put one foot in front of the other.

Stephanie's suitcase didn't arrive in Belfast. She borrowed clothes from her sisters. She never complained. Three weeks after we returned home, we got a phone call from the airport in Salt Lake City, Utah! They had Stephanie's suitcase! It had been to Kuwait in between!

We had been praying it would arrive before a representative from *Open Doors* spoke at our church, because Stephanie's photos of her trip to Mexico were in it and she wanted to show them to him. We were able to pick up her suitcase the evening before he came. Praise God!

Yes, praise our wonderful God, who leads us so lovingly and provides for us so generously!

Amen.

Chapter Seven

September 10, 2023

I mentioned earlier that at the first elders' meeting after our arrival in Cincinnati, the one elder had said that, as long as he was an elder, our debt to our headquarters would never be repaid. After a few years, he moved to another state.

Then one of our ladies died and left a sizeable amount to the church. Some wanted to spend it on improving the property, but I felt it would not be right to do that as long as we owed money to our headquarters. The Director spoke to our church, and a decision was made to send the money to our headquarters to help pay off the debt.

Bob Cload just "happened" to stop at a bank, not his own, to use the ATM and there met (for the first time, I think) another homeschooling father, also far from his home and bank, who asked him if he knew of any pastor who would like to use his set of Financial Freedom videos. Bob immediately thought of me. We watched them in late 1988 and early 1989.

After we watched the video about getting out of debt, Christine Pareigis, now Christine Wagner, asked why we had not repaid our debt to our headquarters, thus propelling us on a journey of faith. I asked the Lord to show us how to repay such a large debt. I think it was around $58,000 at the time.

I recalled that, after the people of Israel were delivered from slavery in Egypt, God told Moses to ask all whose hearts prompted them to give willingly to bring an offering of their most precious possessions, including gold, silver and jewelry, for the building of the tabernacle, the sanctuary where God would dwell among them. (Exodus 25:1-8)

Later we are told: "Everyone who was willing and whose heart moved him came and brought an offering to the Lord for the work on the Tent of Meeting. … All who were willing, men and women alike, came and brought gold jewelry of all kinds: brooches, earrings, rings and ornaments. They all presented their gold as a wave offering to the Lord." (Exodus 35:21-22)

I asked our people if they would be willing to give gold, silver and jewelry, especially anything just lying unused and forgotten about in a drawer, to help pay off the debt.

I emphasized that nobody should feel obligated in any way, and that if our women had inherited jewelry from their mothers and grandmothers and would like to pass it on to their daughters and granddaughters, then that is what they should do.

There was a good response. Gerda Braunheim, who had earlier belonged to our church, kindly priced everything, which we wouldn't have known how to do. These precious items brought in a substantial amount, which was duly sent off to our head-quarters.

One day I found bags of used clothing in my study at the church. When I asked why they were there, I was told, "Oh, they are for the yard sale to help pay off the debt." That was the first I knew about a yard sale! The weather was still cold, so we began praying that the Lord would give us a beautiful spring day for the yard sale.

Finally, the day came and we arranged everything on large tables down on the lower field, close to the main road. The weather forecast had said it would be a nice day, but before any customers arrived, the heavens opened and a heavy rain soaked everything for hours. We had to bring it all up to the house, and Marianne spent hours drying it all.

Then we dropped everything off at a thrift store. The Lord had clearly spoken: "This is *not* how I want you to pay off this debt."

Around that time we owed about $41,000. We decided to have an extra offering once a month for the debt fund. Anyone who wanted to could put something in the baskets as they left the sanctuary. So the debt was slowly coming down month by month.

Early one Monday morning, I went down to the church and saw the signs for the debt fund, which had not been put away from the day before. I felt the Lord was urging me to pray that, if any were considering leaving a gift to the church in their will, they would give it now instead – to help pay off the debt. Then I went up to the house to join the family for breakfast and before long the telephone rang.

It was Clara Auchter, a dear woman in our neighborhood, who was a friend of one of the ladies in our church. She had been brought up as a Lutheran in Germany, but had married a man who had trained to become a Catholic priest, but before his ordination he had been drafted into the German army during World War II. He never did become a priest, but insisted that she should go with him to the local Catholic Church.

She told me, "Later this week you will receive a large gift for the debt fund." I wondered what she meant by a *large* gift. She had earlier given $500 towards paying off the debt, and I wondered if she was going to repeat that, but when the check came it was for $10,000.

We had a deliberate policy of not putting any pressure on our people to give to the general offering or special offerings, and much later I thought, "If we *had* put pressure on the people, maybe they would have given a little bit more, but not $10,000. Only God could do that!"

Every year I had to give a report at our headquarters. For a few years in a row I shared how much we had been able to repay and how much still needed to be repaid. The last time we still owed about $3,000. One of the other pastors asked me to leave the room. When I was called back, I was told that the Synod had voted unanimously to pay the remaining part of our debt, for which we were very grateful. So the last $41,000 was repaid in 41 months. Praise God!

At the time, we didn't realize how important the repayment of the debt was. I will finish the story later in this message.

I had been back on the Parkinson's medication for a couple of years. My neurologist had put me on the standard dosage, but, in retrospect, it was all too much for me. I only averaged about four hours of sleep a night, and the rest of the time I had plenty of energy.

But one day it all caught up with me, and I couldn't face taking the medication anymore. That evening Amy was playing the violin in an orchestra in Indianapolis, about a hundred miles away. There I bumped into Dr. Michael Jacobson, who had been my doctor years before. He advised me not to take any medication for a week and then to see how much I really needed. Instead of three tablets a day, I only needed one tablet every other day, that is, one sixth of what I had been taking. My neurologist suggested that I take half a tablet a day, which has worked out pretty well for more than twenty years now. I take a double dose on Sundays before playing the piano and preaching.

One time Dr. Fredy Revilla, a professor at the University of Cincinnati, stepped in for my neurologist. Instead of the relatively brief visit I had expected, he spent an hour questioning me.

At the end of it all, he told me I have dopamine responsive dystonia, a form of Parkinson's disease, but with a much better prognosis. I am so grateful for the interest he showed and the time he took.

During one holiday season of Thanksgiving and Christmas we faced a number of difficult situations in the church. I prayed that the next Christmas would be much quieter and happier. And God did just that for us! We had a deep snow that froze and couldn't be plowed. So the Christmas Eve service and the Sunday service a few days later had to be cancelled. In fact, we were all alone on our little hill for six days!

One Sunday morning after breakfast, I went down to the church. Suddenly I began to pray that if the Lord wanted me to stay on as the pastor, that day's offering would be the largest one ever. First one family, and then another, and, I think, yet another called to tell me that they would not be coming to church that day. In fact, only 27 people came, which was the lowest number by far that we had had up to that time, and some of them were children. Yet the offering was almost $3,000. I don't know how that happened. All I know is that it did!

I would like to share with you an excerpt from Marianne's diary from Monday, December 24, 2007: "When I was about to go shopping on Saturday, I asked Brian whether I should get a ham for Christmas Day. Tim likes ham. We were not quite sure. So at Biggs I said to the Lord, 'I will get a turkey breast, but if for any reason you feel we should have a ham, would you please give us one? I won't buy one.' So yesterday, Sunday, everyone went to Eden Park to look at the Christmas display. I stayed home alone, because I was very tired. The doorbell rang and someone was tapping on the dining room window. When I opened the door, there was A Risma! [His first name was just the letter A.] He had a package in his arm. He said he wished us a Merry Christmas and gave it to me. It was heavy. I said to him, "This isn't a ham by any chance, is it?" He said, "Yes, it is," and then I told him my little story. He was amazed and laughed with me. When A had left I just rejoiced at how much God was blessing us."

That was dear A's last Christmas, but none of us knew it then. We are sorry to say that he and his family drowned in a typhoon in the Philippines.

We were asked to host a meeting in December 2009. Some would come from our denominational headquarters and others from another city. The back porch of the parsonage was in a very poor condition, just crumbling, and I prayed it would be repaired before the meeting. Our good friend, Aaron Willhite, who lives 125 miles north-west of us, "happened" to come one day, and I asked him if he would be able to repair the worst section, which he did, but then he surprised us by saying he would make us a totally new porch. We rented a dumpster and a jack hammer, and, with the help of our children and other young people from the church, the whole porch was demolished and rebuilt in three days. Aaron even removed the two deep side steps up to the porch and replaced them with three normal sized ones. We were so grateful to him and to the Lord. Aaron's brother, Simeon, and Simeon's Moldovan brother-in-law, Genadi, had painted the outside of our house on another occasion, which was also a wonderful answer to prayer.

In February 2010 the new leadership at our headquarters dissolved our denomination. Churches that had not repaid their debt were sold and the proceeds given to the headquarters.

The churches that *had* repaid their debt were told that they would *not* be given their title deeds. On the Sunday that I shared this with the congregation, Erich Tiepel, Edith Pareigis' brother, was visiting from Colorado. He started investigating and made several calls to the new leadership.

On Thursday, November 11, 2010 a large committee met to discuss our title deed. The majority voted *not* to give it to us.

The next day, Erich Tiepel and I flew to the headquarters and stayed at the home of our good friends, John and Katrina Angeleri. During supper, some who knew about the committee's decision, but didn't agree with it, told us, "There is *no way* they will give you your title deed tomorrow."

The next morning the atmosphere was rather uncomfortable at first, but we just kept quietly committing the situation to the Lord. After a long time someone who had once told me that we would *never* be given our title deed surprised everyone by saying, "When it comes to the vote this afternoon, I will vote that the Cincinnati Chapel gets its title deed." After another long while another person said the same thing.

Then we all went to the dining room for lunch.

Some who had been at the Thursday meeting, but didn't agree with the majority decision, had just arrived for the afternoon vote. They were shaking their heads and saying, "You won't get the title deed." All I could do was whisper, "I think we will."

When they went back for the vote, Erich and I were asked to stay outside. After about forty minutes, they called us in to tell us that they had unanimously decided to give us the title deed.

Praise the God who answers prayer. We love him very much.

Amen.

THE GOD WHO ANSWERS PRAYER

Chapter Eight

September 17, 2023

Today we reach the eighth and last part of the testimony, at least for now. We praise God for all his remarkable answers to prayer. They are not only evidence of his existence, but also of his tender love and care for us. What I share today took place between 2010 and 2017.

During these years the Lord added to our family. On July 2, 2011 Kathy married Luke Stephen Burroughs, and four months later, on November 12, 2011 Amy married Garrett Shay Kuykendall. We are so grateful for our two wonderful sons-in-law, whom we love very much.

Kathy and Luke have given us our three lovely grandchildren. Naomi Elizabeth Burroughs was born on April 17, 2012, Joseph Brian Burroughs on April 25, 2014 and Fiona June Burroughs on June 3, 2016. They are such precious treasures and we love them very dearly.

Many years ago our neighbor to the east of the church property, sold her extensive piece of wooded land to a developer, who wanted to build condominiums. In one day all the trees were cut down. They also excavated a great amount of earth, leaving that property considerably lower than the church's. This exposed the roots of some of our trees on the borderline, causing the trees to die.

In September 2010 we received a letter from the condominium association saying that our dead trees could possibly fall on some of their homes, and asking us to have them cut down. We knew that many companies charge thousands of dollars just to remove one tree, and we needed a number of them to come down. We prayed that the Lord would guide us what to do.

On a Saturday shortly afterwards a few of our young men were willing to try their best, but none of them had ever done anything like this before. We showed them the trees involved, and also mentioned another tree closer to the main road, which was not so urgent. As I looked out of the window, I was surprised to see them walking towards that tree. I prayed whether I should say something and felt I shouldn't. Unknown to us, the Lord was working out everything for the very best.

Someone drove past and saw them trying to bring down that tree. He came back to tell them that they were going about it the wrong way, but that he knew someone with a "cherry picker" who would be able to do it for us. After a while the owner of the cherry picker arrived and told us his story. The Lord knows whether he was telling the truth or not. He said that he had won a lot of money at a casino, and was able to buy the cherry picker for cash, and that was why he charged less than others who still had to make payments on their equipment. He told us he would do everything we needed for $300.

The next day, Sunday, we had an extra offering for the tree removal. It came to exactly $300. I asked the one who had counted it whether he had rounded it up to $300. He hadn't.

A day or two later the owner of the cherry picker and his helper came. They brought down four trees and cut off dead branches from a number of others, and all for only $300.

The following day there was a severe storm from the west, which could have brought down our dead trees on the condominiums. Praise God for his great love and provision!

Our church driveway is exactly one hundred yards long. Over the years its condition had badly deteriorated. From time to time we tried our best to repair the potholes, but it always looked neglected. It was the first impression new people had of our church. Often as we walked or drove up the driveway, we would pray that the Lord would help us to repair or even replace it, but we knew it would be expensive.

One day in 2014, Marion Archer, our treasurer, said that $4,000 of the church funds, possibly more, could be spared for this project.

As the summer was drawing to a close, we called two paving companies to come and give us an estimate.

One day Marianne was just about to drive off to visit a lady who was waiting for her, when a representative of the first company suddenly arrived. He told us that the driveway should really be replaced rather than repaired, but understood that it would be a big expense for a small church like ours. He said he could repair the potholes for $2,250. When Marianne arrived at the lady's home, she explained why she was late, and the lady immediately said, "I would like to pay for that," and gave a check for that amount of money.

Later that day we saw that the man had marked around the potholes with orange paint. We noticed that the areas marked for repair were very skimpy.

So we now had $6,250 available for the project. This made us wonder whether our vision had been too small.

Then the representative from the second company came. He also felt that the driveway should be replaced rather than repaired, and offered us a slightly cheaper price per square foot to repair it.

Unknown to us, one of the ladies in our church had called many contractors, but only one of them, Walter Stogner, came to give us an estimate. We all liked him as soon as we met him. He offered to dig up the old drive-way and replace it for $3.00 per square foot, which was considerably cheaper per square foot than the other two were asking just to repair the potholes.

We asked him if we could begin replacing the driveway from the main road and go up as far as our funds would carry us. He agreed, and we felt that this was the way the Lord was leading us.

The following Sunday I shared all this with the congregation, but that day we didn't have an extra offering for the driveway.

However, the next day a couple called saying that they would like to donate $800 for the driveway, which was very encouraging, and later in the week another couple gave $1,000. So before we had any extra offerings for the driveway, $8,050 had already been given or promised, which was enough to replace the lowest 42% of the driveway. We sprayed a blue line across the driveway to show how much could already be replaced.

After I announced the first extra offering, one man quickly came to me in the foyer and told me that he and his wife would like to give $5,000 to the driveway fund, which, of course, made a huge difference. Another man came out, not knowing this, and told me in no uncertain terms that I should go to the bank the next day and borrow all the money needed and that we could pay it off over time. Having said this, he walked away without giving me a chance to reply, but it already seemed clear to me that God was providing and that we wouldn't need to borrow anything.

Hudson Taylor (1832-1905), the founder of the China Inland Mission, under which my parents-in-law had served, had always emphasized *not* going into debt in order to achieve God's will. He said, "God's will, done in God's way, will never lack God's supply."

That same morning a little girl excitedly told Marianne that she had given two nickels for the driveway fund, which was presumably all she had. This, of course, reminded us of the poor widow who had put two very small copper coins, worth only a fraction of a penny, into the treasury of the temple. Jesus said of her, "I tell you the truth, this poor widow has put more into the treasury than all the others. They all gave out of their wealth – but she, out of her poverty, put in everything – all she had to live on" (Mark 12:41-44).

So at the end of that first extra offering $13,265.10 had been given or promised, enough to replace 69% of the driveway.

Later, one of our ladies told me, "I can only put $5 into the driveway fund, but I wanted you to know that I have at least put something in." This meant a lot to me, especially as some who could've easily given a substantial amount seemed to have decided not to give anything.

That fall a more than usual amount of rain fell, preventing Walter from working on his various projects, including ours. We didn't mind a bit, because that gave us more opportunities to have more extra offerings for those who wanted to contribute. In the end we had seven extra offerings.

One day Marion called to tell me that, instead of using $4,000 of the church funds, we could use $6,000, possibly more. This meant we now had enough funds to replace the lowest 80% of the driveway. We were happy to see the blue line creeping up the hill.

On Wednesday, October 29, Walter came with the two men who would dig up the driveway. We asked them to replace up to the blue line, which was at 84% of the driveway by that time, but Walter was reluctant to do that and felt we should replace the whole driveway. We decided to do what he said and to trust the Lord for the funds still needed.

They had originally hoped to remove the old driveway on Wednesday and to lay down the new driveway on Thursday, but in the end it took them three full days to remove the old driveway because they kept running into problems with their equipment. On Saturday they were able to put down the gravel. We had complete peace because we felt the Lord was giving us one more opportunity to have an extra offering. The next day our people gave another $1,450.

We had asked the men not to lay down the driveway on Monday, because our church building was going to be used as a polling station for the election on Tuesday.

However, on Monday morning, while Marianne and I were at Dr. Fogel's dental office, Amy called to tell us that they were already laying down the driveway. We came home as quickly as we could, because the general offering and the extra offering hadn't been deposited in the bank yet. By the end of the day the asphalting was completed. No one was allowed on it overnight. The next day the election took place with many people driving up and down the driveway – and everything was fine.

Early the next morning, Wednesday, November 5, 2014, Marion brought us the check. In the end $11,590 had been donated and $7,624 came out of the church funds, making a total of $19,214.

Shortly afterwards Walter came, dressed very nicely, and we had coffee and cake together. We talked for about an hour. It was clear that he loved the Lord, and we had sweet fellowship together.

Partway through this project, Marianne and I were reading in the book of Nehemiah. Despite great opposition, the wall around Jerusalem was rebuilt in 52 days. Marianne said to me, "Perhaps the driveway will be completed in 52 days."

And from the first day I mentioned it to the congregation until the day we paid Walter was exactly 52 days. Praise our wonderful God!

When Luke & Kathy bought their home in Mount Healthy, we met their very kind and friendly realtor, Michael Wright, who told us that one day he would find just the right home for us too.

Marianne and I would often walk on the loop around the pastor's house, praying that the Lord would provide us with just the right house at just the right price and at just the right time.

At first we thought we would like to downsize, but the more we thought and prayed about it, the more we felt we would like to have a full basement, a main floor with bedrooms on it and an upper floor for guests. Marianne very much hoped that her siblings would come to visit us, which they did in October 2019. She also wanted room for guests and any of our children, if they needed a place temporarily.

We tried to live on our salary and save our Social Security income (or *Old Age Pension* as it is called in England).

We did visit our families in England and Germany in 2015, most of whom we hadn't seen for many years, but, apart from that, we tried not to touch our savings.

Then on December 12, 2016 Mike Wright sent us an email, saying, "We have a very nice but dated home coming in on Duvall in Mt. Healthy, just around the corner from your daughter. It's a very nice home with a long time owner. It has bedrooms on the [main] and [upper] floors. Homes on the street sell for around $100,000, but this one may be in the mid 90s or upper 80s due to being dated. I haven't seen it, but have a feeling it would be just what you are looking for."

It wasn't on the market yet, but Mike arranged for us to see it at 11 o'clock on Monday, December 19. Unfortunately Kathy couldn't join us because she had to feed Joseph, who was almost 8 months old at the time, but Mike introduced Marianne, Luke and me to Mr. James Kemper, who had lived there since it was built for him by his brother in 1961. We all loved the house, and when Marianne saw Mr. Kemper's "man cave," she said, "Oh, Brian, this will be your study," which it has been ever since. (We were able to change some of the dated features and are content to live with the rest.)

Mike said, "We'll make a first offer of $87,500." Mr. Kemper immediately accepted it. Mike said to us, "I think he thought, 'These are the people I want to live in my house.'"

The house was inspected, and when Mike read the report, he made a short list of things Mr. Kemper should see to, but Mr. Kemper said, "I'm too old to see to these things. I will reduce the price by $3,000." So the price was now $84,500.

We noticed that Mr. Kemper was using a walker (following a knee replacement operation) and still had a lot of work to do to empty out the house – all alone because his wife had died – so I suggested that instead of the closing date being 30 days away it could be 60 days, but Mike suggested 45.

I hadn't thought of this, but this way we got one more Social Security payment. The closing fees were $422, so the final amount we had to pay was $84,922. With the extra Social Security payment we had enough to pay cash. Without it we wouldn't have.

By God's grace, we bought the house at just the right time. Within a year the prices had almost doubled, and they have continued to rise since then.

Praise God for his wonderful provision!

Sometime later, our dear friend, Kevin Wagner, whom we would soon lose to cancer, helped us with the electric box and other things, for which he would only accept a small part of what we wanted to pay him.

The Lord continues to answer prayer, even in amazing ways, but we'll leave it at this, at least for now.

Sometimes I say, "Lord, you are the God of the threepenny bit (Andrew), the £70,000 (the OM ship), the 700 pesetas (the Spanish village), the £5 note (Lionel and Audrey), the £90 (my return to Iran), the $400 (Mike Litteral), the $10,000 (Clara Auchter) and the rest of the debt fund, the $300 (the tree removal), the $19,000 (the church driveway), the $85,000 (our house) and so much more. I know you will continue to look after us."

I want to end by repeating what I said at the beginning of this testimony: "Rosalind Goforth (1864-1942) saw many answers to prayer when she and her husband were missionaries in China, but she said, 'This doesn't mean that we haven't failed in many ways, because we have.' I want to echo that.

The Lord has been very gracious to me [and us], answering so many prayers in such remarkable ways, but that doesn't mean I haven't failed in many ways, because, sad to say, I have."

All praise to our wonderful God, who leads his people so lovingly and provides for them so well.

Amen.

A little note about our children:

Kathy is a stay-at-home mom, who, along with Luke, homeschools their three children. They live just around the corner from us.

Since 2012 Stephanie has lived and worked in various countries in Europe, presently in Ireland.

From 2007 to 2009 Amy served on Operation Mobilization's ship, the *Doulos*, visiting 14 countries in south-east Asia and Australasia. Amy & Garrett live 6 miles from us.

From 2013 to 2019 Timothy was on active duty in the United States Navy, where he served in naval aviation as an aircrew loadmaster on a cargo aircraft. He visited 50 countries. He lives 3 miles from us.

From 2015 to 2020 Emily lived in Nürnberg, Germany, where she studied International Business. She now works in London, England as an accountant.

Appendix One

The Message of the Three Crosses

written 2010, printed 2011

The following account is taken from the Holy Bible, the Gospel of Luke, chapter 23, verses 32-33 & 39-43.

The other men, both criminals, were also led out with [Jesus] to be executed. When they came to the place called the Skull, there they crucified him, along with the criminals – one on his right, the other on his left. ...

One of the criminals who hung there hurled insults at him: "Aren't you the Christ? Save yourself and us!"

But the other criminal rebuked him. "Don't you fear God," he said, "since you are under the same sentence? We are punished justly, for we are getting what our deeds deserve. But this man has done nothing wrong."

Then he said, "Jesus, remember me when you come into your kingdom."

Jesus answered him, "I tell you the truth, today you will be with me in paradise."

Almost two thousand years ago, when Jesus Christ and two criminals were nailed to three crosses, the greatest drama this world has ever seen was being acted out.

On the central cross, Jesus Christ was dying for us, the innocent for the guilty, bearing the punishment for our sins, so that all who would believe in him would be forgiven and receive the gift of everlasting life.

To the one side of him was a guilty criminal, who remained unrepentant, unbelieving and unforgiven. When he died later that day he perished in his sins.

On the other side of Jesus was an equally guilty criminal, but one who repented, believed and was forgiven. Before the sun set that day his spirit was in paradise with the Lord Jesus.

The fact is, the cross of Christ divides all humanity into two groups: those who are everlastingly saved and those who are everlastingly lost.

Many centuries before Christ, Isaiah, in his great prophecy about the atoning death of the coming Messiah, had written, "he ... was numbered with the transgressors" (Isaiah 53:12).

And only the previous evening Jesus had quoted this to his disciples.

He said, "It is written: 'And he was numbered with the transgressors'; and I tell you that this must be fulfilled in me. Yes, what is written about me is reaching its fulfillment" (Luke 22:37). In the eyes of many that day Jesus was regarded as a criminal who deserved the death penalty, rather than as the Lamb of God who was taking away the sin of the world (John 1:29), bearing our sins in his body (1 Peter 2:24).

The two criminals were almost certainly associates of the notorious Barabbas, who had been "in prison with the insurrectionists who had committed murder in the uprising" (Mark 15:7)

"It was the governor's custom at the Feast [of the Passover] to release a prisoner chosen by the crowd" (Matthew 27:15). Pontius Pilate wanted to release Jesus, but wicked men stirred up the crowd to demand the release of Barabbas and the crucifixion of Jesus. The cross on which Jesus Christ died had almost certainly been intended by the Roman authorities for Barabbas.

The infamous place of execution was called Golgotha (Matthew 27:33), which meant "The Place of the Skull" in the local language of Aramaic. We know it better as Calvary, from the Latin word for skull.

Crucifixion was the most terrible, dreaded and shameful form of capital punishment in the ancient world. The suffering was intense and prolonged. Often people lingered on for two or three days, because death did not come from loss of blood but rather from heart failure.

The crucifixion of the innocent Jesus was the darkest deed ever committed on this earth.

In the other gospels we are told that, at first, **both** of those crucified with Jesus "heaped insults on him" (Matthew 27:44 & Mark 15:32). The one criminal kept up his hateful abuse. "Aren't you the Christ? Save yourself and us!" He was asking Jesus to deliver him from the physical horrors of crucifixion. He wanted Jesus to save him from the *consequences* of his sins, but not from the sins themselves, otherwise Jesus would have gladly saved him too.

Later the Apostle Peter wrote, "'He committed no sin, and no deceit was found in his mouth.' When they hurled their insults at him, he did not retaliate; when he suffered, he made no threats" (1 Peter 2:22-23). When the other criminal saw how Jesus responded to all the verbal abuse, he had a change of heart.

He repented of his terrible sins, and tried to bring his fellow criminal to repentance too. "Don't you fear God," he said, "since you are under the same sentence?" By this he meant, "You are going to die very soon. You will have to give an account of your life to a holy God, a righteous Judge. So don't persist in your sins, but repent and cast yourself on the mercy of God."

He continued, "We are punished justly, for we are getting what our deeds deserve." He openly, humbly, acknowledged his own great guilt. He did not make any excuses or justify himself in any way. He confessed that he deserved the death penalty, even death by crucifixion.

We may or may not have committed the same sins as these men, but the Bible declares that each one of us stands guilty before God. It says that "*all* have sinned and fall short of the glory of God" (Romans 3:23) and that "the wages of sin is death" (Romans 6:23). If we also do not make any excuses for our sins or justify ourselves in any way, but humbly and openly admit that we too deserve to be punished for our many sins, then we too can experience God's incredible mercy.

The repentant criminal not only pointed out that they were getting what their deeds deserved, but also that "this man," Jesus, had "done nothing wrong." In the previous hours a number of other people had also testified to Jesus' complete innocence. Judas Iscariot was seized with remorse and said, "I have betrayed innocent blood" (Matthew 27:4). Pilate's wife "sent him this message: 'Don't have anything to do with that innocent man'" (Matthew 27:19). Pilate himself said, "I have examined him in your presence and have found no basis for your charges against him. Neither has Herod, for he sent him back to us; as you can see, he has done nothing to deserve death" (Luke 23:14-15).

The Apostle Paul later explained the great transaction that had been taking place on that central cross: "God made him who had no sin to be sin for us" (2 Corinthians 5:21). Jesus was bearing the awful punishment for our sins in his sinless body.

The repentant criminal cast himself entirely on God's mercy, which is the only basis for eternal salvation. He said, "Jesus, remember me when you come into your kingdom." Pilate had had "a notice prepared and fastened to the cross. It read: Jesus of Nazareth, the *king* of the Jews" (John 19:19)

This repentant man understood that Jesus, although right then suffering the agonies of death, would one day rule over a kingdom, and that he himself, although totally unworthy, wanted to be included in that kingdom. This world has seldom seen such daring faith!

All the time that Jesus was on the cross, he ignored all the abuse coming at him from all sides, but when this contrite man cried out for mercy, Jesus quickly and graciously responded with the greatest words of forgiveness and hope ever spoken, *"I tell you the truth, today you will be with me in paradise."* This was a wonderful fulfillment of a promise Jesus had made earlier, "Whoever comes to me I will never drive away" (John 6:37).

At three o'clock in the afternoon Jesus "bowed his head and gave up his spirit" (John 19:30). Then the legs of both criminals were broken to hasten their deaths (John 19:32). Shortly after the violent blow, at the moment of death, the spirit of this repentant criminal went straight to paradise to be with Jesus Christ, the one who had paid the penalty for his sins.

From this remarkable incident many wonderful lessons can be drawn:

1. All who are saved are saved only by God's grace and mercy.

This man was saved only because of God's great love and totally undeserved mercy. This is God's only way of salvation.

"God our Savior ... saved us, not because of righteous things we had done, but because of his mercy" (Titus 3:4-5).

"For it is by grace you have been saved, through faith – and this not from yourselves, it is the gift of God – not of works, so that no one can boast" (Ephesians 2:8-9).

2. No one is saved by his or her own good deeds.

This man had broken both God's law and society's laws. He had wronged many people, and had no time or opportunity to make restitution or to turn over a new leaf. He was in no position to perform any meritorious deeds or to run on any errands of mercy because his hands and feet were nailed to a cross. He had done nothing to deserve salvation, nor could he earn it. But then no one has ever been saved by his or her own good deeds anyway.

"All our righteous acts are like filthy rags" (Isaiah 64:6). We too cannot earn salvation through our own good deeds, nor can we even help God to save us. It is only through what Jesus Christ did for us on the cross that we can be saved.

3. No one is saved through baptism or any other religious ceremony.

Because this man was nailed to a cross, it was impossible for him to be baptized or to perform any other outward religious act, and yet he was completely forgiven and assured, *"I tell you the truth, today you will be with me in paradise."* Sometimes, for various reasons, it is not always possible for people to be baptized. Yet God never intended that baptism or any other religious ceremony should save, or even contribute towards the salvation of, anyone. Salvation is only possible because Jesus Christ paid the penalty for our sins. He is the only Savior. We cannot save ourselves by performing religious rituals.

4. At the moment of death the spirits of the saved go straight into the presence of the Lord.

Jesus did not say to this man, "Because your sins and crimes have been so great, you must first suffer the fiery torments of purgatory, so that you can be purified and made ready for heaven." No! Purgatory is not even mentioned in the Bible. Jesus paid the *full and complete* penalty for our sins, and nobody can, or needs to, add anything to his perfect work.

Jesus said to him, *"I tell you the truth, today you will be with me in paradise."*

Before the sun set that very day, at the moment his earthly life was over, and before his body was laid in the grave, his spirit soared into the presence of the Lord.

The Apostle Paul later wrote, "I desire to depart and be with Christ, which is better by far" (Philippians 1:23), and "We … would prefer to be away from the body and at home with the Lord" (2 Corinthians 5:8)

5. **As long as there is life, it is still possible to be saved.**

This man, in his final hours upon this earth, truly repented of his sins, and was promised by Jesus, *"I tell you the truth, today you will be with me in paradise."*

And all others who truly repent of their sins, even at the last possible moment, will also experience God's mercy. While there is life, there is hope. It is never too late to sincerely cry out to God for his gift of everlasting life.

However, in no way should this encourage anyone, foolishly or presumptuously, to put off the matter of his or her eternal destiny until the last possible moment. We do not know how our end will be. Some are unexpectedly struck down in a moment – through accidents, strokes or heart attacks – and then it is too late. We only have this present moment. The Apostle Paul wrote, "I tell you, *now* is the time of God's favor, *now* is the day of salvation" (2 Corinthians 6:2)

6. God gives the assurance of salvation to those he saves.

Not only was this man gloriously saved, but he was also completely assured of his salvation. There was no doubt about it, because Jesus promised him, *"I tell you the truth, today you will be with me in paradise."* Jesus could not have made it any clearer. Such an assurance is a wonderful part of the gift of salvation, bringing great peace to our souls.

The Apostle John later wrote these wonderful words, "This is the testimony: God has given us eternal life, and this life is in his Son. He who has the Son has life; he who does not have the Son of God does not have life. I write these things to you who believe in the name of the Son of God so that you may *know* that you have eternal life" (1 John 5:11-13).

7. **In order to be saved, each person needs to respond in the same way the repentant criminal did.**

From their crosses one criminal went to heaven, while the other went to hell. Not everyone will be saved. What is going to happen to *you*?

It is not until we see the guilt of the repentant criminal as a picture of our own guilt before God that we too will cry out, "Jesus, remember me."

If, like the repentant criminal, we realize we are guilty before God, if we are truly sorry for the grief our sins have caused to God and others, and if we have determined to turn away from continuing in those sins, then, as we cast ourselves on God's infinite mercy, he will gladly receive and forgive us.

If this man was not beyond the reach of God's mercy, then neither is anyone, no matter how great his or her sins may be.

The Apostle Paul wrote these urgent words, "We implore you on Christ's behalf: Be reconciled to God" (2 Corinthians 5:20). I, too, implore you to cry out to God, sincerely and in your own words, for his mercy and salvation, because "everyone who calls on the name of the Lord will be saved" (Romans 10:13).

Appendix Two

Are You Aware That ... ?

September 25, 2022

Unfortunately, many people are not aware of what the Bible teaches about some very important matters, yet everyone has the right to know, because it will affect everyone.

Are you aware that the Bible teaches that just before the greatest time of suffering comes upon the earth (that is, the tribulation), Jesus Christ will come again to take away to heaven all who belong to him?

The apostle Paul taught, "For the Lord [Jesus] himself will come down from heaven, with a loud command, with the voice of the archangel and with the trumpet call of God, and the dead in Christ will rise first. After that, we who are still alive and are left will be caught up together with them in the clouds to meet the Lord in the air. And so we will be with the Lord forever. Therefore encourage each other with these words." (1 Thessalonians 4:16-18)

And the Lord Jesus himself promised, "I will also keep you from the hour of trial that is going to come upon the whole world to test those who live on the earth [that is, the tribulation]." (Revelation 3:10)

Are you aware that the Bible teaches that a seven-year-long period of tribulation (described in detail in the book of Revelation) will then come upon all who are left upon the earth?

The Lord Jesus warned, "For then there will be great distress, unequaled from the beginning of the world until now – and never to be equaled again. If those days had not been cut short, no one would survive." (Matthew 24:21-22)

Are you aware that the Bible teaches that the Antichrist (controlled by Satan) will rule the earth during the tribulation?

The apostle John wrote, "[The false prophet] made the earth and its inhabitants worship the [Antichrist]." (Revelation 13:12)

and

"[The false prophet] forced everyone, small and great, rich and poor, free and slave, to receive a mark on his right hand or on his forehead, so that no one could buy or sell unless he had the mark, which is the name of the [Antichrist] or the number of his name. This calls for wisdom. If anyone has insight, let him calculate the number of the [Antichrist], for it is man's number. His number is 666." (Revelation 13:16-18)

Are you aware that the Bible teaches that all your own good deeds and religious practices are not enough to bring you safely to heaven?

The prophet Isaiah tells us, "All our righteous acts [our best efforts] are like filthy rags [in God's sight]." (Isaiah 64:6)

And the apostle Paul explained, "For it is by grace you have been saved, through faith – and this not from yourselves – not by works, so that no one can boast." (Ephesians 2:8-9)

and

"He saved us, not because of righteous things we had done, but because of his mercy." (Titus 3:5)

There is only one sane response to all this:

The Lord Jesus said, "Here I am! I stand at the door [of your heart] and knock. If anyone hears my voice and opens the door, I will come in and eat with him, and he with me." (Revelation 3:20)

And the apostle John wrote, "To all who received him, to those who believed in his name, he gave the right to become children of God." (John 1:12)

So do not trust in all your own good deeds and religious practices to bring you into heaven. Rather, trust that what Jesus Christ did on your behalf (bearing the punishment for your sins in his sinless body when he died on the cross) is sufficient to save you forever.

Then, when the Lord comes for all who belong to him, you will not be left behind to go through the tribulation (the seven-year-long battle between God and Satan).

Rather, you will be rescued from the greatest time of suffering ever to come upon the earth.

You could pray something like this:

"Lord, I am so sorry for all the sins I have committed against you and others, and I ask you to forgive and cleanse me, so that when you come for all who belong to you, I will be taken to be with you and not have to go through the great suffering that will come upon the earth. In Jesus' name. Amen."

Made in the USA
Monee, IL
05 December 2024

70923437R00085